Unfolding the Eightfold Path: A Contemporary Zen Perspective documents the author's study of the Fourth Noble Truth, from his first encounter as a young man, throughout his life as a Zen practitioner, and into his elderhood.

This work presents a unique interpretation of the dynamic nature of the "right" elements of right view, thought, effort, concentration, mindfulness, speech, action, and livelihood. Nine distinctive explanations for each of the elements explore an evolutionary view of their dynamic change from conceptual knowledge to liberating thought.

With astute clarification, this work offers an in-depth view for engaging the Eightfold Path at any stage of a practitioner's experience. It offers a map for the transformational outcome of dedicated study, practice, and integration of the Fourth Noble Truth.

Unfolding the Eightfold Path demonstrates how to create coherent order out of the insights of a lifetime of practice.

Unfolding the Eightfold Path:

A
Contemporary
Zen Perspective

Unfolding the Eightfold Path:

A
Contemporary
Zen Perspective

DALE VERKUILEN

FIRETHROAT PRESS LLC
MADISON, WISCONSIN

Copyright 2014 © by Dale Verkuilen
All rights reserved

Published by Firethroat Press, LLC
2789 Marledge Street
Madison, WI 53711-5257
Web: www.firethroatpress.com
Email: info@firethroatpress.com

ISBN: 978-0-9830972-3-5

Library of Congress Cataloging Number: 2013938851

Publisher's Cataloging-In-Publication Data
Publisher's Cataloging-In-Publication Data
(Prepared by The Donohue Group, Inc.)

Verkuilen, Dale, author.
Unfolding the Eightfold Path : a contemporary Zen perspective / Dale Verkuilen.

pages : illustrations ; cm

Includes bibliographical references.
ISBN: 978-0-9830972-3-5

1. Eightfold Path. 2. Four Noble Truths. 3. Spiritual life—Buddhism. 4. Verkuilen, Dale—Religion. I. Title.

BQ4320 .V47 2014
294.3/444   2013938851

Cover design and graphics:
Aaron Gilmore, www.gilmoreart.com

Printed in the United States of America.

*To the memory of Teruko Hosokawa (1918-2004)
For communicating to me the world of the Brahma Viharas
without ever mentioning them.*

"Zen Masters have said that in complete perfect enlightenment there are eighteen great awakenings and countless minor awakenings. A Zen proverb says, 'Those in a hurry do not arrive.'"[1]

Table of Contents

Note to Reader i
Acknowledgments iii
Preface 1
Chapter 1: The Eightfold Path Chart 5
Chapter 2: Commentaries on the Triads 15
Section 1: Foundations of Zen Buddhist Practice 19
  Triad 1P
    Study 21
    Practice 27
    Ethical Conduct 35
  Triad 1U
    Spiritual Autonomy 41
    Absolute Equality 45
    Intimacy 51
Section 2: Inquiry as the Central Point of Practice 55
  Triad 2P
    Questioning 57
    Impartiality 61
    Relating 67
  Triad 2U
    Introspection 73
    Insight 79
    Interconnection 85

Section 3: Establishing and Cultivating Psychological Well-being ... 91
  Triad 3P
    Personal Orientation ... 93
    Intrapersonal Orientation ... 99
    Interpersonal Orientation ... 105
  Triad 3U
    Psychological Maturity ... 109
    Embracing ... 115
    Dignity ... 121

Section 4: Establishing Awareness of "Don't-Know Mind" ... 125
  Triad 4P
    Inevitability ... 127
    Clarity ... 133
    Integrating ... 137
  Triad 4U
    Discernment ... 141
    Immediacy ... 145
    Mystery ... 149

Section 5: Refining and Living Liberation ... 155
  Triad 5
    Sustenance ... 159
    Wholeheartedness ... 165
    Authenticity ... 171

Eightfold Path Summary ... 177
Endnotes ... 179
Bibliography ... 187
Glossary ... 191
The Eightfold Path Charts ... 199
Other Offerings from Firethroat Press ... 207
About the Author ... 209

Note to the Reader

Full-size copies of the Eightfold Path Charts are available as a free download at www.firethroatpress.com/downloads.

Acknowledgments

Many thanks:

To the Madison and Dubuque Sanghas for helping refine the material presented in this book.

To Sheryl Lilke for counseling, editing, and many ideas that improved the book's readability.

To Kira Henschel at HenschelHAUS Publishing for expertise in book design and layout.

To Aaron Gilmore at Gilmore Art for cover design.

To Troy Couillard & Tom Breuer for advanced reading and commentary.

And to my wife Renshin Barbara: her support and suggestions animate every page of this work.

—Dale Verkuilen

Preface

When I was in my twenties, I came across my first book on Buddhism. It laid out the Four Noble Truths[2] in the conventional manner, ending with the Fourth Noble Truth of the Eightfold Path. I was left with an appreciation of the Buddha's logical expression of his teaching, especially his systematic approach to the problem of suffering. However, in spite of the Buddha's methodical strategy, the full implication of the Four Noble Truths' importance escaped me at the time. I missed the way to apply the teaching, resulting in no practical outcome. Later, by other means, I became acquainted with the practice of Zen meditation and initiated a lifetime study with a series of teachers. An introspective analysis of the Four Noble Truths was left on the rear burner to simmer while I focused on learning how to meditate. Thus, I, like many others, acquired the fundamentals of Buddhism through a hit-and-miss manner of attending Dharma talks, self-study, and absorbing insights from fellow practitioners.

Many years later I was invited to give a series of Dharma talks to a Buddhist group that was getting organized. Information on Zen flowed out with alacrity, but I soon recognized something more was required for many beginners. Where do you begin with newcomers? Of course it's the Four Noble Truths, and especially the practicality of the Eightfold Path. My attempt to create a detailed guidebook showed me I lacked the ability to articulate what exactly the Four Noble Truths meant to me. This deficiency prompted several years of reflection and writing to establish a firm understanding of what my experience over the years actually included. This book is the result of that period of internal exploration.

A common accounting of the Eightfold Path consists of listing the eight elements—right view, right thought, right effort, right concentration, right mindfulness, right speech, right action, and right livelihood—and describing how they function. Many excellent renditions are available that provide an in-depth analysis of each element. Some of them acknowledge that maturity in practice earns a diligent practitioner a developed sense of the right elements. As a practitioner grows within the Dharma, the elements manifest in varying ways according to one's level of experience. For example, the right view of the beginner is not the same as that of a practitioner of twenty years. This is true for all other elements as well.

The reflective examination of my years of practice revealed a number of stages or sections of the Eightfold Path that I had experienced. At the outset of my practice, I dealt with integrating the basic information and insights. The right elements defined themselves appropriately for that assortment of circumstances. As time went on, further efforts established observation and inquiry as central to my practice, resulting in a whole new set of "right" definitions. This pattern of change went on for forty years and produced a number of sets of right elements, each of which expressed a unique perspective particular to a unique stage of my spiritual development. As my practice matured and my understanding of the teaching deepened, I found that the first set of right elements was not replaced by the generation of the

Preface

second set. Rather, the first set was incorporated into the second set and so on, producing, when viewed as a sum, a holographic image of how the right elements manifest, interact, and evolve in the course of a lifetime of practice.

The Fourth Noble Truth of the Eightfold Path exemplifies the practical means to directly experience the truth of the first three. The First, Second, and Third Noble Truths are vivid torches of Buddhist teaching. They are like a white light focused through a prism producing the colors of the rainbow from red to violet. However, the first three Noble Truths do not generate colors; they produce the array of the eight right elements.

Continuing with this metaphor, colors that emanate from a prism are not discrete; they blend from red to orange to yellow and so on without distinctive lines of demarcation. The right elements are similar. They are not separate functions, existing apart from each other. The boundary between the elements cannot be found. The prismatic colors are a wondrous, continuous expression of light's makeup; the right elements are equally descriptive in portraying the unique uninterrupted relationship from one element to the next. Practice over the years fleshed out the right elements from a set of concepts to an inclusive, complementary collection that includes foundational teachings, mature insights, and the linking stages in between.

During Zen practice, many of the perspectives encountered in Zen seem at cross-purposes or unrelated when viewed as independent occurrences. Yet, when reviewing their place in retrospect, entirely different meanings and associations become apparent. Reflecting on events from afar reminded me what space shuttle astronauts realized while orbiting above the vast expanse of the Eurasian continent. They observed lightning bolts produced by storms that were separated by vast distances. These bolts

Unfolding of the Eightfold Path

occurred with an unexpected synchronized timing, a viewpoint not perceivable by observers within the individual storms. The observers on the ground could not witness the immediate relationships of the widespread weather patterns. They assumed the individual storms they were observing acted independently. Without distance, the interconnections between the storms remained unknown. And so it is with many life events: they seem to stand on their own, but in truth many unseen interconnections exist. In the study of Zen, practice over a long period of time provides the means to unveil heretofore hidden aspects of seemingly disconnected life long internal and external relationships.

The Eightfold Path, as presented here, offers a frame of reference similar to the astronauts viewing the relational synchronicity of apparently isolated lightning storms. The inherent interconnections of the various aspects of our lives come to be seen as intricately and positively related. Viewing these previously unnoticed or barely acknowledged relationships replaces old habits of thought with new understandings of intimate communications with the world of nature, other people, and, ultimately, the internal dialogue of Zen practice.

Chapter 1
The Eightfold Path Chart

The Eightfold Path Chart (see the Chart at the back of the book) that will be introduced in Chapter 1 and used as a reference throughout this book presents a summary view of the results of my reflections on how the Eightfold Path unfolded within my practice over the years. The chart contains expressions of common experience as well as idiosyncratic features. It is not meant to be authoritative. It attempts to document the progression of possible changes as practice matures.

The chart provides what I conceive as a holographic image of the Eightfold Path, because, like a hologram, it provides several viewpoints at one time. The chart encapsulates a large amount of information. At first glance, it may appear impenetrable with its many components. However, once you learn its fundamentals, a structure that organizes practice becomes available.

The Eightfold Path Chart shows the relationships between the sections, triads, and right elements. The following paragraphs describe these elements and explain how they operate and relate to one another. Taken together, the sections, triads, and elements convey a picture of the Eightfold Path's transformative nature.

Unfolding of the Eightfold Path

THE FIVE SECTIONS OF THE EIGHTFOLD PATH

The Five Sections shown on the Eightfold Path Chart are a way of grouping Buddhist teachings into an experiential understanding of the three Buddhist categories of wisdom, meditation, and morality.[3] Each of the sections represents one of the phases of study and practice that occur chronologically over the course of a lifetime. They include the information about the form and outcome of the teaching of that section. The sections start with the basics of Zen practice, advance through what is encountered when following the path, and offer descriptions of experiences one may have along the way.

- **Section 1: Foundations of Zen Buddhist Practice**
  "Foundations" provides initial motivation to begin the practice of Zen, the means and methods to stabilize meditation practice, and introduces the universal teaching of Mahayana Buddhism.

- **Section 2: Inquiry as the Central Point of Practice**
  "Inquiry" establishes the focal point that leads to an inspired breakthrough. It asks us to view our daily life dilemmas and the issues surrounding them as opportunities for spiritual growth. Inquiry includes all aspects of human investigation: scholastic knowledge, introspective understanding, and experiential wisdom.

- **Section 3: Cultivating Psychological Well-being**
  "Psychological Well-being" creates the solid base that supports Buddhist practice. It teaches the path of living that generates and sustains a balanced approach toward spiritual endeavor while fulfilling the duties of daily life.

Chapter 1: The Eightfold Path Chart

- **Section 4: Establishing Awareness of "Don't-Know Mind"**
  "Don't-Know Mind" is the mind of nonduality. The study of nonduality comprehends inconceivability as the heart of all experience. It is the practice/realization of zazen that uncovers the ordinary and natural way of being in the world.

- **Section 5: Refining and Living Liberation**
  The teachings of the four preceding sections become combined through an unwavering and long-standing cultivation of "Don't-Know Mind." The result is a life based on an accurate discernment of the facts of life—one imbued with trust and confidence, the attributes of Buddhist faith.

Over several decades of my practice, each section evolved in time, one after the other from Section 1 to Section 5. Once a section developed and was understood, the next one began to open and became the center of my attention. When that section's main message was comprehended, awareness of the next section arose. The new section did not supplant the previous one. Its meaning served as the basis for deeper understanding of what was to come. The initial encounter of a section's meaning was only the beginning of engagement with that particular teaching. I experienced each section numerous times, and each encounter presented an opportunity to discover different aspects of significance.

The Triads

The term "triad" means a group of three. On the Eightfold Path Chart, triad refers to the three major teaching points of Buddhism. Each triad shows the unified action of wisdom, meditation, and morality[4] for the particular subject being addressed.

Unfolding of the Eightfold Path

The Eightfold Path Chart is organized into nine triads that describe the maturation of the right elements. Each triad is made up of the three categories. The categories consist of the following elements:

1. Wisdom = right view and right thought
2. Meditation = right effort, right concentration, and right mindfulness
3. Morality = right speech, right action, and right livelihood.

Each triad has a heading, a subheading, and an explanation for each of its right elements. The headings are the titles of the category. The subheading helps define the name of that triad's category, and the definitions of the right elements provide the details of the meaning of each element for that specific category.

	Wisdom	**Meditation**	**Morality**
Triad 1P Personal	**Study** Reading/ Reflection/ Reasoning	**Practice** Mental Discipline	**Ethical Conduct** Precepts
	Right View	Right Effort	Right Speech
	Right Thought	Right Concentration	Right Action
		Right Mindfulness	Right Livelihood

For example, the heading for the wisdom category of Triad 1P is Study. The definition of Study is expanded in the subheading as Reading, Reflection, and Reasoning. Then the elements for Study—right view and right thought—are defined (see chart). Unique definitions of each right element are given for each category of each triad producing nine perspectives for each right element.

Chapter 1: The Eightfold Path Chart

Triads 1–4 are paired triads; the one labeled with "P" expresses the personal aspect of the section; the other marked with "U" the universal side. For example, Triad 1P refers to the personal aspect of Section 1, Triad 1U to its universal aspect. The same is true for the triads of Sections 2, 3, and 4. Two triads are necessary for the first four sections because they require working with the personal and universal aspects of awakening as discrete entities, hence two triads per section. Section 5 needs only one triad because it displays complementary nondual activity: the unified activity of the personal and universal.

The triads are parts of a section of teaching, and have special internal and coupled interactions. Understanding these relationships and working with them acknowledges that the personal and universal aspects are of equal importance, and must be simultaneously understood and developed. Both the personal and universal must be dealt with. The two aspects act interdependently, with an equal level of consequence.

Personal awakening seeks individual liberation, addressing one's distinct and unique requirements. It acts primarily on personal karma, the components of the self that condition an individual's personality. Personal karma has its roots in culture, education, nurturing, volitional acts, and the immediate environment. The ideal is the Arhat, an individual who achieves the goal of personal awakening. Generally speaking, the teachings for the personal aspect of awakening follow the Buddhist analysis and teaching of what constitutes the self.

Universal awakening recognizes the interconnection of all beings. It addresses the collective and ultimate characteristics of the seeker. It acts on universal karma. Universal karma is defined as the shared action of the universe conditioning an individual's life, arising from the extensive actions of those presently living and

Unfolding of the Eightfold Path

as well as all antecedent beings. The ideal of universal awakening is the Bodhisattva, one who dedicates his or her life to the spiritual liberation of all beings. The teachings for the universal aspect of awakening are the perspective of the Mahayana tradition.

Learning the personal without the universal deprives one of the fullness of one's insight. Attempting to learn the universal without a firm grounding in the personal leaves one vulnerable to the possibility of not having the introspective tools to sustain the experience of a breakthrough. Without the universal, the personal tends toward the moralistic and scholastic; without the personal, the universal lacks emotional connection and stability. Taking them together moves us toward a more complete understanding of idiosyncratic and shared spiritual issues.

How the Triads Function

The practice of Buddhism formally begins when a person encounters the Dharma and recognizes the truth of the Buddha's teaching of the Four Noble Truths. This is taking the first step on the path—right view. All else flows from that initial insight. The first triad, and all subsequent triads, start at right view and develop through to right livelihood. The development within each of the individual triads follows the pattern contained in the following list:

Wisdom

1. Right view: A new way of seeing the world becomes apparent and brings about new directions of thought.

2. Right thought: The new directions of thought reveal previously unseen interconnections. New intentions are formulated that conform to the latest view.

Chapter 1: The Eightfold Path Chart

Meditation

3. Right effort: The will is activated to correspond with one's new intentions.

4. Right concentration: New insights are experienced within the impartial stillness of the Informal Mind—Formal Posture.

5. Right mindfulness: The new insights are expressed within the composed movement of the Formal Mind—Informal Posture.

(See the commentary on Triad 1P Practice page 27, for explanation of Informal Mind—Formal Posture and Formal Mind—Informal Posture.)

Morality

6. Right speech: Language is recognized as the path to the liberation of thought.

7. Right action: Dignified conduct expresses the truth of Buddha's teaching.

8. Right livelihood: Authentic personhood is expressed in selfless service.

THE ELEMENTS OF THE EIGHTFOLD PATH

The order and descriptions of the right elements in this book vary from the orthodox explanations found in the Pali Canon. The descriptions of the right elements maintain most of the traditional understanding, but their order is modified to capture the flavor of Western experience.

The conventional order places right speech, action, and livelihood before right effort, concentration, and mindfulness. Traditionally, ethical concerns are considered the basis of a meditation practice. In the East, morality comes first, then meditation.

Unfolding of the Eightfold Path

However, in the West, practitioners do not have the benefit of growing up in a Buddhist culture. They learn principles of Buddhist morality within meditation practice. This is the reason right effort, concentration, and mindfulness are placed ahead of right speech, action, and livelihood. The right elements listed and studied this way mirrors how many (probably most) Westerners advance in their Zen practice.

The definitions listed below are general statements about the right elements. They contain the fundamental understanding of the elements used in this study. They amplify the usual descriptions. The brief characterizations are the starting points for a growth in clarity.

- Right view—Perspective that acknowledges the truth of the human condition

- Right thought—Resolve to follow the path of awakening

- Right effort—Focus of the will on being present in the moment

- Right concentration—Meditation in stillness

- Right mindfulness—Meditation in movement

- Right speech—Recognizing the liberating relationship of thought and language

- Right action—Responding with wholeheartedness

- Right livelihood—Unencumbered activity, liberation, authenticity

SYNONYMS FOR "RIGHT"

The Madison, Wisconsin and Dubuque, Iowa Sanghas of the Midwest Soto Zen Community developed synonyms for the

Chapter 1: The Eightfold Path Chart

adjective "right" during discussions of the Eightfold Path. They expanded its meaning beyond the dualistic framework of right and wrong. The class participants were encouraged to offer introspective understanding of their engagement with the "right" of the elements. What follows are suggested synonyms:

- Correct—Seeing without elaboration
- Accurate—Coherence of intention
- Appropriate—Activity in harmony with conditions
- Constancy—Maintained effort
- Beneficial—Valuable and constructive
- Precise—Clearly expressed understanding
- Complete—Wholeheartedness
- Sustaining—Effort that nourishes
- Resonant Response—Rapport with what is
- In Accord With—Moment-by-moment awareness
- Subtle Inspiration—The unity of tranquility and insight
- Lucent—Illuminating with clarity
- Natural—Without shame or blame
- Integrity—Unembellished conduct

Each synonym invites a practitioner into an expansive experience. Thorough and skillful reflection using the synonyms as guides produces an unconstrained and non-dogmatic approach to engaging openly with the elements. The ability to grasp the overall viewpoint of the list gives "right" a practical basis in addition to the usual cognitive understanding and offers an experiential understanding of the various interpretations.

Chapter 2
Commentaries on the Triads

"If you will only leave behind false conditioning, you will be 'such' like the Buddha."[5]

Zen Master Chinhul

The commentaries on the triads and their categories that make up the body of this book describe the five sections and nine triads in more detail. They are not meant to be definitive; I offer the triads as an organizational groundwork for reflection and insight.

The nine triads are each made up of the three categories of wisdom, meditation, and morality—resulting in twenty-seven accounts of the unfolding of the Eightfold Path. They indicate the progression from the foundational teachings to established abilities.

The triads begin with Study—Practice—Ethical Conduct, progress through seven additional triads, and culminate in the unified triad of Sustenance—Wholeheartedness—Authenticity. Each triad presents the development of a mini path that originates in the motivating force of right view through to the resulting rectitude of right livelihood. Studying each triad individually promotes the understanding of the ideas it conveys, and provides the basis for taking on the next triad. In this step-by-step method, one advances through the triads and sections.

Unfolding of the Eightfold Path

Triad	Wisdom	Meditation	Morality
1P	Study	Practice	Ethical Conduct
1U	Spiritual Autonomy	Absolute Equality	Intimacy
2P	Questioning	Impartiality	Relating
2U	Introspection	Insight	Interconnection
3P	Personal Orientation	Intrapersonal Orientation	Interpersonal Orientation
3U	Psychological Maturity	Embracing	Dignity
4P	Inevitability	Clarifying	Integrating
4U	Discernment	Immediacy	Mystery
5	Sustenance	Wholeheartedness	Authenticity

Even though the Eightfold Path itself, plus the appended commentaries, seems to be an application of a formulaic method, I urge you to resist the temptation to consider the information in that way alone. Rather, make an effort to uncover the internal relationships between the sections, triads, and the triads' categories and attempt to see them as a whole. Doing so unveils a far greater aid to understanding than approaching them only by the step-by-step process.

The triads maintain their dynamic nature throughout life, maturing and revealing new insights; one is never finished with their individual and collective study. Repeatedly the individual triads provide unforeseen pathways to an enriched conscious

Chapter 2: Commentaries on the Triads

relationship with the unknown. The relationships between the triads contain subtle differences beyond the common view. With diligent engagement one realizes them to be intriguing, filled with opportunity, sometimes surprising, and always sustaining.

Section 1
Foundations of Zen Buddhist Practice
Introduction to Triads 1P and 1U

It takes an unusual mind to undertake the analysis of the obvious.

Alfred North Whitehead

In the first two triads that comprise Section 1, we encounter the fundamentals of Zen practice. Triad 1P, Study—Practice—Ethical Conduct, contains the basic teachings of the personal view of the Eightfold Path. Triad 1U, Spiritual Autonomy—Equality—Intimacy, introduces the universal principles of Mahayana Buddhism. Gaining an understanding of these triads will give you a firm grounding in the fundamentals of Foundations from the personal and universal sides.

Triad 1P describes what is contained in the approach and practice of the teachings of personal awakening. The main points of the triad are:

- Establishing the truth of the Buddha's teaching of the Four Noble Truths within our life
- Learning the discipline of meditation practice

Unfolding of the Eightfold Path

- Establishing a moral life that has the Buddhist precepts at the heart of daily activities

Triad 1U contains the main principles of Mahayana Buddhism. They emphasize the teachings of universal awakening:

- Emptiness—the view that all forms are impermanent and lack an enduring self-nature.
- All life is interdependent.
- All phenomena express universal truth.

The personal and the universal teachings when taken together constitute the oneness of Zen Buddhist practice and understanding. They express the inclusive and holistic principles of Buddha's teaching. Whitehead's "unusual mind" is the mind that hears the Dharma and commits to the "analysis of the obvious." The Eightfold Path provides the instruction on how we take on the "analysis of the obvious" and penetrate its mystery.

Triad 1P – Personal
Foundations
Wisdom[6]

Study:
Reading/Reflecting/Reasoning

"To study the Buddha Way is to study the self."[7]

Zen Master Dogen

Right View: Directly experiencing the validity of the Four Noble Truths.

Right Thought: Forming the intention to gain experiential understanding of the Buddha's teachings on awakening.

Triad 1P: Study

The study of Buddhism begins when an individual encounters the possibility of awakening. Becoming aware of this stream of teaching opens a path not recognized before. Awakening requires the study of all aspects of the self. This is frequently begun as an intellectual undertaking, and then eventually evolves to consider the more subtle aspects of self. Here we will begin consideration of the Buddha Way, which most often begins with reading and expands from there. Embarking on a study of Buddhist literature and historical figures builds a strong foundation.

The right view of Study is accepting the veracity of the Four Noble Truths. It starts with the truth of *dukkha*—suffering arises—the first of the Noble Truths. Looked at from a wider perspective, however, dukkha consists of the direct experience of the human situation with all its complexities.

In Western culture, because the teaching of awakening is not part of our tradition, it can appear strange when first encountered. But that was not always the case in other cultures. In ancient India, committing oneself to the search for truth was considered admirable. A lifelong path of personal development that regarded awakening as the ultimate destination was commonplace. The journey began in youth with an intellectual commitment to study, and was followed in adulthood by a wholehearted engagement with the karmic life of a householder. The reward of living to elderhood was a one-pointed effort to obtain liberation. This model of study-karma-liberation afforded every opportunity for living each stage of life intently and completely, bringing about the greatest good for oneself, one's family, and society at large. The different stages of this exemplary life are not separated in three clean-cut sections. When one is a youth, karma and liberation are important, but study and developing an intellectual grounding in the teachings maintain center stage. The same relation exists in adulthood and the retirement years. In adulthood and elderhood, resolving karmic issues and achieving liberation are accentuated respectively, but study continues throughout life. For the most part, this model avoids confusion over one's changing roles and provides a clear path to liberation. The three major elements of the responsible life are given the opportunity to mature, each in their own time.[8]

This model of study-karma-liberation contains fundamentals useful for the modern Buddhist lay-life, a primarily non-monastic practice. It offers the opportunity to create the means to adapt the Buddha Way into our culture of college, blended families, and corporate employment. When we understand how to incorporate the three necessities of the path to enlightenment, the barriers that are thought to exist between Zen Buddhist practice and our everyday life are minimized. The model of study-karma-liberation values universal literacy, acknowledging the great value the many years of schooling bestow upon us. Cultivating continual learning comes easier with the fondness and inclination toward reading and reflection that our upbringing supplies. Assuming we come into contact with the knowledge of the way of awakening, possess ample conceptual learning skills, and have the will to follow the path, all the essential means are at our disposal for acquiring the principles of Buddhist practice.

The Buddha spent his life expounding the Dharma, but he always insisted that the truth of his teaching had to be validated by each person individually through his or her own efforts and experience. As Zen Master Dogen points out in the Genjo Koan[9], the study of the Buddha Way begins with the indispensable study of the self. The powers of examination are brought to bear, employing reading, reflection, reasoning, and memory to develop the knowledge of how the self functions.

Triad 1P: Study

Securing the vantage point of cognitive awareness is the first step on the Eightfold Path: the development of right view and right thought. When we test this new awareness in the world, we challenge unexamined assumptions. Without inquiry into the nature of these assumptions, we remain unconscious and uncertain. With a dedicated study, starting with cognitive awareness, developing a purposeful intention, and adding the direct experience of meditation, the fruits of Study can be realized.

Triad 1P – Personal
Foundations
Meditation

Practice
Discipline

To give your sheep or cow a large, spacious meadow is the way to control him.[10]

Zen Master Shunryu Suzuki

Right Effort: Applying the will in an appropriate, useful, and consistent manner.

Right Concentration: Learning about our inner makeup and how to deal with its complexities. Learning and applying the principles of Formal Posture—Informal Mind.

Right Mindfulness: Applying the learning from the meditation practice into the world of daily activities. Learning and applying the principles of Formal Mind—Informal Posture.

Triad 1P: Practice

The prominence of the systematic approach to meditation in Zen Buddhism is one of the factors that make it unique. Meditation is at the heart of the inquiry into the nature of self. Feelings of dissatisfaction (dukkha) power our initial cognitive inquiry. However, without sitting down and engaging in the transformation of meditation, we stay trapped in our conceptual view of the world, chasing ourselves in circles. When we incorporate a regular meditation practice into our daily lives, we begin to leave that endless entanglement behind. The mental discipline of meditation practice contains the means to connect with the deep aspects of our makeup. In Practice, one learns how to observe and experience the inner world in new ways. Positive change is the result of this process.

The practices of concentration and mindfulness are characterized differently in other styles of teaching. Don't be confused by the variety of explanations you encounter in your study. Consider all of them tentative until your own definitions become clear. This book describes right effort, right concentration, and right mindfulness using certain terms and definitions. They are an attempt to create a practical understanding of how to value and expand what we learn while sitting. In this way, over time, meditation and daily life become a seamless whole.

Right Effort

As right view sets the stage for the establishment of wisdom, right effort provides the means to transform a conceptual outlook into the Buddhist vision of the self. Interconnection to the visceral truth of Buddhist philosophy becomes alive and powers our subsequent endeavors. At first, right effort in meditation practice can lack consistency. Beginners have the tendency to lose the thread of momentary existence. However, continued exertion overcomes that tendency and a continuity of awareness is established. Diligence and courage are the characteristics of right effort.

Right Concentration

Right concentration consists of Formal Posture and Informal Mind operating in harmony. Formal Posture refers to a prescribed sitting posture: one that is precise yet completely natural. Informal Mind is a container for all thoughts and views, an awareness that has no limits or boundaries. Right concentration is achieved within a balanced mind.

Formal Posture

Formal Posture is the bedrock of meditation practice. Getting comfortable with the posture opens the doors to concentration. The Formal Posture of sitting meditation uses a cushion that promotes straight-back sitting. The cushion should be thick enough so that the hips are higher than the knees. Accomplishing this will allow the spine to assume its natural curvature, and quite naturally the center of gravity is established in the lower abdomen. The ears should be over the shoulders and the nose in line with the navel. The lips and teeth should both be shut, while the eyes remain half open, cast downwards. Breathing should be through the nose filling the belly during inhalation. The hands should be folded in the lap just beneath the navel forming an ellipse with the thumb-tips slightly touching. If the hands are folded correctly, all weight will be removed from the shoulders. Use a lap pillow if your hands need support to ensure no tension builds up in your neck and shoulder muscles. The chin should be tucked in slightly.

Although this posture may seem arbitrary, it is the product of thousands of years of human endeavor. Practicing it will reveal the vigor, intensity, and comfort that are its nature.

Triad 1P: Practice

Informal Mind
The Informal Mind is Suzuki Roshi's "spacious meadow." The mind becomes relaxed and alert, without limitation or definition. Mental formations within the mind come and go without preference. However, a keen awareness of the mental formations' life cycles from their arising, existence, and dissolution is established and cultivated. We witness our mentality as vast, fleeting, and interdependent.

The practice of Informal Mind consists of tranquility and insight. Tranquility grows out of the continuity of awareness achieved over time. Insight occurs spontaneously within the sphere of tranquility. Neither need be sought. They naturally arise within the consistent, persevering right effort of meditation practice.

Our minds are filled with thoughts, fantasies, internal conversations, memories, anticipations, worries, confusions, doubts, feelings of joy or sorrow, fears, and so on. The Informal Mind maintains a continuity of awareness of all of the inner activity, along with the environmental stimuli, without drifting into a dream world. When you lose the thread of attention to the moment, simply start the observation once more without recourse to judgment or analysis. Conscientious practice over time will limit the distractions. There are no shortcuts to gaining powers of concentration; one must practice. The breath serves as an aid for staying in the moment. Counting breaths can be helpful. Just following the breath is more difficult. But it is an effective means to remain present; simply place your attention on the breath and watch it come and go.[11]

Right Mindfulness
Right mindfulness consists of Formal Mind and Informal Posture. Formal Mind refers to a mental attitude: one that is precise yet

completely natural. Informal Posture means freedom of movement permeated with awareness. Movements of the body are freely responsive to the needs of the moment and are in harmony with the awareness of the Formal Mind. Right mindfulness means expressing a balanced mind.

Formal Mind
In zazen, one develops continuity of awareness. The Formal Mind of right mindfulness is this continuity in action. The Informal Mind of sitting is a mind without boundaries, one that lets all mental elements exist within the stream of awareness; the Formal Mind of movements in the world maintains a continuity of awareness of all physical activities and mental events as they occur. The Informal Mind focuses on a mentality without boundaries for the internal world; the Formal Mind focuses on a mentality without boundaries for the external world. We cultivate awareness of each movement with a minimum of distraction; when distraction does occur, we return awareness to the moment without judgment.

Informal Posture
Informal Posture is our daily life activity within the awareness of Formal Mind. It is learned in the meditation hall by attentive participation in the many training procedures and then extended into all aspects of daily life. An example of this training is walking meditation. Slow, attentive walking teaches us how to transition from the quiet mind of sitting meditation to the outer world of motion. The minimal physical movements of walking require only that we stay in line, permitting the mind of sitting meditation to fill our awareness as we walk.

The practice of Informal Posture consists of physical movement and engagement with the world permeated with tranquility and insight. The continuity of awareness of sitting becomes the mind of walking. The mind of sitting becomes the Formal Mind that is at the heart of the liberated activities of Informal Posture.

Soyu Matsuoka Roshi, my first Zen teacher, instructed beginners to practice for six months before they considered what changes their meditation may have brought about. He asserted that it takes time for the mind to settle down and for one to notice any differences. In this way, the experiential results of Zen meditation are emphasized from the beginning. An example of the efficacy of this teaching is contained in a comment by a practitioner of our Sangha. She said she does not recognize any change when sitting, and wonders what all the fuss is about. Then she gets up and realizes that her conceptual and emotional worldview is different from what it was thirty minutes ago. The power of self-awareness to effect real change cannot be overestimated.

Triad 1P– Personal
Foundations
Morality

Ethical Conduct
Precepts

Right Speech: Refraining from lies or slander, using appropriate timing, not being harsh or insulting, cultivating kindness.

Right Action: Establishing and maintaining daily activities to promote the health and welfare of oneself and others.

Right Livelihood: Engaging in work that does not harm others.

Unfolding of the Eightfold Path

The Sixteen Buddhist Precepts

The Three Vows of Refuge
Taking refuge in the Buddha
Taking refuge in the Dharma
Taking refuge in the Sangha

The Three Pure Precepts
Do not create evil
Practice good
Actualize good for others

The Ten Grave Precepts
Affirm life—do not kill
Be giving—do not steal
Honor the body—do not misuse sexuality
Manifest truth—do not lie
Proceed clearly—do not cloud the mind
See the perfection—do not speak of others' errors and faults
Realize self and other as one—do not elevate the self
and blame others
Give generously—do not be withholding
Actualize harmony—do not be angry
Experience the intimacy of things—do not defile the
Three Treasures[12]

Triad 1P: Ethical Conduct

The Buddhist precepts are not the equivalent of the commandments of Judaism and Christianity. They do not attempt to impose restrictions on behavior given by some outside authority, nor are they moral imperatives. However, when first encountering the precepts, most Westerners see them in a restricted moral sense; our ways of thinking on these matters are deeply ingrained. As we work with the precepts and witness our lives unfolding within them, the effects of the teachings slowly penetrate. The precepts are transformed from moral dictates to guides to an awareness of the Buddha mind. The precepts are descriptions of the world of a buddha, awakening expressed in daily life.

"Precept" in Sanskrit is *Sila*, one meaning of which is to form a habit. Habit as a precept means to take on vows to behave in certain ways. In Buddhism, vows can seem unattainable because they are looked at from the point of view of one life. The Buddhist understanding of vow transcends one life. Making a vow goes beyond the limitations of the moment, of the day, of a personal lifetime, introducing the eternal. When realizing this, the vast world of Buddhist action reveals itself. Acting in accord with the precepts is accepting the truth of Buddhahood, even when we do not yet fully understand what that means. Dainin Katagiri Roshi proclaims, "The main purpose of Buddhism is to form the habit of practice as a vow forever. This is just taking a journey in the universe, day by day, step by step."[13] Considering this statement, a vow, the habit of practice, the embracing of the precepts as a way of life, provides refuge and is the beginning of the end of confusion and anxiety. What is a vow? It is an entryway into the vast aspect of our universal life. Katagiri Roshi taught that our limitations were not our problem; instead it is our relationship with vastness.

As was stated earlier, Morality was placed at the end of the triads. This was done to indicate that Ethical Conduct—right speech, right action, and right livelihood—is a natural outcome of successful engagement with the principles of Study and Practice. It is also true that

Unfolding of the Eightfold Path

correct Ethical Conduct provides positive enhancement for our continuing efforts in Study and Practice.

What follows is Bodhidharma's version of the Ten Grave Precepts. Their tone and definition are different from the precepts listed above because they arise from the Mahayana teachings. One can recognize how the teachings of the Mahayana enlarged the point of view from the original formulation. Bodhidharma's vision ties them directly to the awakened mind and the universal view of the Mahayana teachings. He begins each statement with "Self-nature is clear and obvious," meaning the following precept comes from an abiding wisdom of the true nature of self. The first precept is a good example. Not killing evolves from an affirmation of life to a realization that because of the interdependent nature of existence, if one questions the meaning and results of killing, extinction cannot be found. The previous set of precepts interprets them through the personal mind; this second set offers the universal perspective.

THE TEN GRAVE PRECEPTS (BODHIDHARMA'S VERSION)

1. Self-nature is clear and obvious. In the sphere of everlasting Dharma, not nursing a view of extinction is called the precept of refraining from killing.
2. Self-nature is clear and obvious. In the sphere of unattainable Dharma, not having a thought of attainment is called the precept of refraining from stealing.
3. Self-nature is clear and obvious. In the sphere of unstained Dharma, not yielding to attachment is called the precept of refraining from committing adultery.
4. Self-nature is clear and obvious. In the sphere of inexplicable

Triad 1P: Ethical Conduct

Dharma, not speaking a single word is called the precept of refraining from telling lies.

5. Self-nature is clear and obvious. In the sphere of originally pure Dharma, not being ignorant is called the precept of refraining from intoxicants.

6. Self-nature is clear and obvious. In the sphere of the flawless Dharma, not speaking of others' faults is called the precept of not speaking of the faults of the four kinds of members of the Sangha.

7. Self-nature is clear and obvious. In the sphere of non-discriminating Dharma, not distinguishing oneself from others is called the precept of not praising oneself or slandering others.

8. Self-nature is clear and obvious. In the sphere of all-pervading true reality Dharma, not arousing greed is called the precept of not begrudging the Dharma or materials.

9. Self-nature is clear and obvious. In the sphere of the ego-less Dharma, not making the ego real is called the precept of not being angry.

10. Self-nature is clear and obvious. In the sphere of the undivided Dharma, not arousing a dualistic view of sentient beings and Buddha is called the precept of not slandering the three treasures.[14]

Both sets of precepts contribute value to one's practice. The personal and universal descriptions may appear contradictory, but Zen teaching requires immediate understanding of complementary activity of the particular and the collective. In one's life this manifests as a shared natural process where the personal and universal aspects give rise to an inclusive wholeness of being.

Triad 1U – Universal
Foundations
Wisdom

Spiritual Autonomy
Alone in the World

*"When you know for yourself that something is good and beneficial when undertaken, continue that practice.
When you know for yourself that something is harmful and causes suffering when undertaken, cease that practice."*[15]

Shakyamuni Buddha

Right View: Understanding the nature of personal responsibility.

Right Thought: Recognizing Emptiness as the medicinal that resolves the adverse effects of conditioned states.

Triad 1U: Spiritual Autonomy

Spiritual Autonomy, the universal aspect of wisdom of Foundations, builds on its predecessor. In Study, groundwork of cognitive understanding and familiarity with Buddhist historical figures, texts, and methods is established. In Spiritual Autonomy, this foundation is strengthened and expanded.

During his travels, the Buddha was approached by a group of people known as the Kalamas. They had encountered many spiritual teachers. When hearing the Buddha was nearby, they asked to receive instructions. He gauged their understanding and need, providing them with the instruction quoted above. These seemingly simple words can easily be overlooked, but when they are examined closely they expose our life circumstance. The phrase "know for yourself" appears twice in the teaching. It is the key to grasping the meaning of Spiritual Autonomy.

A Dharma sister of mine once asked her teacher, "What about the ultimate aloneness?"

He replied, "You do not accept this?"

No one likes to have a serious inquiry followed by another question, yet in the end it proved to be the stepping-stone to understanding the principle of Spiritual Autonomy and the life direction it generates.

The "ultimate aloneness" exchange is similar to the one between the Kalamas and the Buddha. The Kalamas wanted to know what the Buddha's teachings were and they were given appropriate help. The Zen student wanted clarification and direction on her experience of aloneness. She was new to Zen at the time, but unlike the Kalamas, she recognized aloneness to be at the center of her experience.

My Dharma sister's teacher responded with a question whose meaning encouraged her to develop her experience of ultimate aloneness. What she discovered as she did so was the ground where all seekers stand: we are born alone, live alone, and die alone, and no one has say-so over us at any time. We may put ourselves into situations where we voluntarily relinquish our will to others to learn something from them, or we may have our outer freedom taken from us and be put into a prison. But "know for yourself" can never be given or taken. Ultimately, our life as it unfolds is our teacher—the only true authority. Accepting aloneness helps define our relationship to the self, and is the basis for meaningful actions. Is aloneness nihilistic or pessimistic? It can be viewed that way, but it is acknowledging the world just as it is.

    The clear perception of aloneness and accepting it as a fact of existence is the right view of Spiritual Autonomy, an acknowledgement that leads to a resolute understanding of the relationship of inner authority and our sense of self. Gaining a stable view of "who is in charge" opens the mind to its true nature. Right thought takes a practitioner past rigid views into emptiness, where nothing has a permanent and independent existence, where everything is interconnected.

    Immanuel Kant proclaimed that the eighteenth century European Enlightenment was mankind's escape from "self-imposed tutelage." In other words, men had wrapped themselves in a mental straitjacket, submitting to outside authorities to interpret truth. The Enlightenment denied any external power as legitimate, considering reason as the master arbitrator. Reason alone provided the way to intellectual freedom.

    Similarly, an individual who takes up the practice of Zen has the chance to remove the existential bonds of conditioned states and attain spiritual liberation. In Zen, emptiness is the understanding that clarifies spiritual obstructions. Realizing emptiness frees one from the entrapment of conditioned states. It teaches us how to work to free ourselves within the vast web of existence. The nature of the world ceases to be confining, and is met with as a pathway to freedom.

Triad 1U – Universal
Foundations
Meditation

Absolute Equality
Alone in the World with All Beings

"If I have the least shred of concern for my own spiritual progress, I must care–really care–for the spiritual growth of even the grass."[16]

Francis Cook

Right Effort: Intentionally acting in a way that recognizes that all life is interdependent and equal.

Right Concentration: Acknowledging the birth of compassion for oneself.

Right Mindfulness: Acknowledging the birth of compassion for others.

Triad 1U: Absolute Equality

Absolute Equality explores the experience of "alone with all beings." The state we experience as aloneness acknowledges the fact that we live a separate existence and are in the end not able to share directly any thought, feeling, or emotion experienced by another. When we mistakenly presume that this separate self is the complete and only way of being, however, we are met with trouble and turmoil. Aloneness does not stop there, for ultimately all beings are in this exact situation no matter what their form or level of intelligence. Even though we are cut off from directly sharing the content of our experience, we all possess the common feature of "alone with all beings" and find Absolute Equality within that realization.

The practice of zazen operates as a powerful tool for cultivating recognition of equality. Throughout our lives most of our conventional education encourages us to embrace dualistic thinking, an emphasis that sets us apart from the rest of the world and ensures the legacy of the subject-object split. In the tranquility and insight of zazen, the mind of interdependence replaces our closely held misunderstandings of separateness.

Absolute Equality is a radical way of seeing that grows and develops right in the center of the chaos of daily life. "Alone" combined with "all beings" is interdependence, and as Francis Cook states, "I must care—really care—for the spiritual growth of even the grass" points out the way to do this.

Earlier in the twentieth century Aldo Leopold, the seminal environmentalist, adopted a formula, later known as the "Golden Rule of Ecology," on how to correctly relate to the world. He stated:

> "A thing is right when it tends to preserve the integrity, stability, and beauty of the biotic community. It is wrong when it tends otherwise."[17]

Unfolding of the Eightfold Path

Leopold experienced Earth as an intimate community that could not be pulled apart into fragments, analyzed, and acted upon without the whole of the biosphere being affected in some way. His awakening to the close weave of existence was precipitated in his youth in an encounter with a dying wolf.

Leopold was living in Arizona and regularly hunted near his home. On one hunt, Leopold's party shot a she-wolf and her cubs because fewer wolves on the mountain meant more deer for human hunters. Leopold later recounted his experience: "We reached the old wolf in time to watch a fierce green fire dying in her eyes."[18] Witnessing the "fierce green fire" began a reflective time for him that ultimately opened up a new view on the nature of relationships that previously had escaped his understanding.

The extermination of wolves from the mountain allowed the deer population at first to expand, matching the hunters' wishes. However, in time, because of the increased population, over-browsing occurred, killing all the brush and trees. With the plants gone, mud eroded off of the mountainside into the streams and rivers, killing the water plants, fish, and other aquatic animals. With the destruction of the brush, the small animal population decreased, forcing most of the raptors and other predators to find new territories. In the end, the deer population also declined because of a lack of food. The mountain became barren, whereas before the shooting of the wolves, a rich habitat of flora and fauna lived in balance and harmony. The lesson was not lost on Leopold. He understood that killing the wolves killed the mountain as well.

Leopold devoted his life after this awakening to teaching and writing about the intimate relationship of all beings within Earth's biological community. He is said to be the father of the environmental movement. Similarly, each person who consciously touches the web of intimate relationships, like Leopold, becomes

Triad 1U: Absolute Equality

a father or mother of balance and harmony within the realm of their influence. The barrenness of personal isolation from the immediate surroundings disintegrates and is replaced by a vision of the interdependence of all forms of life. No one can fully comprehend the extent and effects of "zazen [that] is one with all existence and permeates all time."[19] Every act of goodwill and generosity is like one drop of water striking the calm surface of a pond, setting off an endless stream of beneficial ripples.

Triad 1U – Universal
Foundations
Morality

Intimacy
Rapport with All Beings

*"So studying the boundlessness of activity is
studying the self.
This is called intimacy."*[20]

Dainin Katagiri Roshi

Right Speech: Using words and tone of voice that acknowledge the power of everyday communication.

Right Action: Practicing and performing our daily pursuits within the awareness of the needs of others.

Right Livelihood: Expressing our commonality of being within our occupations, family lives, and other endeavors.

Triad 1U: Intimacy

In *The Secrets of the Blue Cliff Record*, Case 19, "Fingertip Zen", the compiler, Setcho, proclaims in the introduction, "When a single flower is picked up, the whole earth is contained in it."[21] In this statement, he introduces us to the spirit of Intimacy.

When we practice zazen, we pick up the single flower and study it closely. This examination witnesses our internal, as well as the reality of our external, relationships. Setcho says the whole world is contained in the flower. Becoming aware that the single flower of our self, or the flower of any other being, contains the whole Earth begins to build a view where we enter into deep familiarity with the world as it unfolds. The study of the boundless activity of zazen centers on learning how to become aware of the universal truth of interdependence that manifests in all phenomena. Dogen consistently points out that zazen is exactly this awareness. In the Jijiyu Zammai (King of the Samadhis) he encourages us to see zazen's ultimate value. "…when even just one person, at one time, sits in zazen, they become imperceptibly one with each of all the myriad things…"[22] We may first come to this view in zazen, but that understanding eventually permeates all our thoughts and activities.

When I was just beginning my practice, I approached my first teacher to inquire whether he would accept me as a student and what I might expect if he did so. We were in his apartment, and after tea, a snack, and a light chat, I got up the nerve to ask him what he considered essential in Zen practice. He answered without hesitation, "Heart-to-heart communication." Further questioning at that time as to what he meant by that yielded nothing of consequence. The words and descriptions ceased, and the path to Zen experience commenced. Later, after we had lived together for a number of years, a mutual friend asked him how we were getting along. His response was, "The only things

I have of my own are my socks." What happened during that time to bring about that degree of closeness? Not much except commonplace encounters. Nothing dramatic, nothing outwardly profound. Nonetheless, our common effort to penetrate the core of Zen teaching slowly molded our relationship.

I would like to relate another example of how boundless study opens one to intimate concerns for self and other. Recently I became reacquainted with a person I practiced with thirty years ago. Once during a sesshin we attended together, he wept intermittently for three days. Over coffee after the sesshin, I asked him what was the cause of the tears. He explained that the tears arose from a feeling of self-forgiving compassion for himself. Within that feeling many judgments he had about his previous behavior dropped away. Then later the compassionate insight grew to include the other sesshin participants, expanding to a circle of empathetic concern. The experience left him with a new outlook on how compassion dispels notions of preference and limitation.

Years later we met and reminisced about the old days, touching on this shared sesshin. I asked him what long-term effect, if any, the weeping experience had on him. He said it thoroughly changed him, offering him a new way to form meaningful relationships. It became the pivot point of his Zen practice, out of which there arose the confidence to accept a position of leadership in a Zen community. He is now leading several groups, and it is apparent from the genuine respect his students afford him that he has successfully made the opening of compassion for self and others central in his life and teaching.

My friend's life demonstrates how intimacy is cultivated. It is the meeting place where our interests and actions unite with the needs and wishes of our companions.

Section 2
Inquiry as the Central Point of Practice
Introduction to Triads 2P and 2U

He who asks the questions cannot avoid the answers.

Proverb from the Cameroon

During the long history of the genus Homo, curiosity about the world served to bring about significant changes in the way proto-humans responded and adapted to the challenges of their environment. The sustained probing and subsequent innovations resulted in increased cognitive abilities that eventually led to Buddha's rediscovery of the spiritual and moral nature of the universe. The Buddha and his followers devised many unique and powerful methods that nurtured that understanding. None were as powerful as curiosity's mature cousin—inquiry.

Inquiry transforms curiosity from a hit-and-miss adventure into a conscious tool for exploration, one that acts directly with, and on, the imaginative and creative segment of the human makeup. Formulation of the great questions, coupled with determination, is the necessary ingredient of an inspired breakthrough.

Unfolding of the Eightfold Path

From the Buddha down to the present day, inquiry has been the focal point of practice. The Buddha questioned why there is suffering in the world. This encapsulated the essence of his spiritual quandary. Buddhist practitioners who apply his teachings witness the clarity of their own spiritual dilemma as it emerges from a persevering inquiry. Doing so, we walk along with the ancients and become intimate with the teaching trail they left for us.

Triad 2P, Questioning—Impartiality—Relating, explains how to move past identification of thought as the self. It introduces a revolutionary means of connecting with the world.

Triad 2U, Introspection—Insight—Interconnection, confirms what was understood in Triad 2P, and provides the means to expand personal insight into a universal vision.

Triad 2P – Personal
Inquiry
Wisdom

Questioning
Conditioned States

"Accumulate learning by study, understand what you learn by questioning."[23]

Zen Master Mingjiao

Right View: Valuing the dilemmas that our life situation brings to us.

Right Thought: Placing questioning at the center of our practice.

Triad 2P: Questioning

In Study we accumulate learning; in Questioning we observe the process and content of our inner world. Practitioners of zazen are reoriented from submissive acceptance of the world to active participation in the conscious unfolding of life. The basis for a questioning attitude is to pay close attention and not take anything for granted. A questioning attitude undermines the tendency to allow inner and outer events and circumstances to occur and recur without notice, subsequent articulation, and intentional action. Questioning works directly with the substance of our life and directs us to ask, "What is really going on?"

Beginning practitioners notice the impermanent and independent nature of the thinking process. Before taking up zazen, most often they regarded themselves as being in control of their thinking. However, this assumption is almost immediately compromised as they begin to notice that their thoughts come and go, mostly apart from volition. They discover that their mental life consists mainly of habitual patterns of thought and affect that arise from pre-existing conditioned states. When an environmental stimulus triggers a conditioned state, the habitual response connected with that state appears within the mental landscape. Needless to say, it is a disturbing insight to learn that the majority of our personal experience surfaces from an ever-changing web of causes and conditions. We do not easily rouse ourselves from the erroneous supposition that an ever-present fully formed awareness and will is completely in charge.[24]

Learning the myriad ways conditioned states function requires a mind rigorously schooled in observation and questioning. Zazen practice provides the ability to monitor conditioned states in action, and to describe their composition and operation.

The right view of Questioning values the existential dilemma of our situation. It is a call to action, an opportunity that

Unfolding of the Eightfold Path

sharpens awareness of the operation of conditioned states, and how that conditioning plays out. Working with conditioned states, rather than ignoring them out of hand, enhances their significance and usefulness. Life dilemmas portray embedded conditioned states. Questioning and penetrating the nature of a dilemma helps foster a wider view into the nature of our conditioned states, and their problematic consequences.

Right thought creates paths of action that are practical and based on direct experience, not preformed assumptions. I am reminded of a time I witnessed a clear example of one Zen teacher's understanding of this point. She was facilitating a discussion after a presentation on Zen and instruction for zazen practice she gave to a group at a Catholic college. Not surprisingly, the fundamental Christian question of belief in God came up, sparking a sharp debate. The Zen teacher listened to the rapid-fire back and forth responses. After a while, when a quiet moment arose, she gently offered her commentary, "Whether you believe in God or not, your problem is still your problem." This sums up Zen's point of view on practice: belief structures will never satisfy; they will only create emphasis on differences. Questioning encourages study, and activates the confidence to "know for yourself."

Triad 2P – Personal
Inquiry
Meditation

Impartiality
Balance without Preference

*"The Great Way is not difficult for those who have
no preferences.
When love and hate are both absent everything becomes clear
and undisguised.
Make the smallest distinction, however, and heaven and earth are
set infinitely apart."*[25]

Zen Master Kanshi Sosan

Right Effort: Putting aside the mundane concerns of daily life at the onset of zazen practice.

Right Concentration: Allowing conditioned states to become apparent within the Informal Mind.

Right Mindfulness: Observing with the Formal Mind the effects of conditioned states in everyday relationships.

Triad 2P: Impartiality

The skill of observing the rise and fall of the effects of conditioned states is the basis of the ability to maintain a continuity of awareness during zazen. In the practice of Informal Mind, the various contents of the mind stream are allowed to arise and subside without interference. An impartial awareness notes the occurrence of whatever is happening. Impartiality means not interdicting the flow in any way—neither chasing pleasant experiences nor running away from those that are disagreeable. Learning to see events as they occur just as they are without judgment or involvement allows us to identify the barriers that stand in the way of our continuity of awareness.

Impartiality is part of the second phase of what Dogen calls learning "the backward step that turns your light inwardly to illuminate yourself."[26] The first phase is a mind that goes from one thought or mood to another without awareness. "Turning your light inwardly" establishes conscious awareness with the heretofore-automatic flow of conditioned states. Dogen explains in the Fukanzazengi, "Cease all the movements of the conscious mind, the gauging of all thoughts and views."[27] This means to set aside our involvements and concerns of the moment, separating the self from the habitual identification with our usual mental patterns. The issues of daily life, however, do not go away just because we turn our attention away from them. Rather, they exist in the background. Temporarily freeing the mind from conscious involvement with the conventional world makes room for other mental activity. Later in the Fukanzazengi, Dogen offers direction on how to proceed in zazen: "Think of not-thinking. How do you think of not-thinking? – Nonthinking."[28] This seemingly enigmatic advice, when unbundled, connects the practitioner with Kanshi Sosan's "no preferences," Tung-shan Liang-chieh's "turning

Unfolding of the Eightfold Path

away and touching are both wrong," and Steve Hagen's "longing and loathing." From ancient to contemporary times the message is the same.

Dogen's not-thinking is observation of the internal world without making distinctions about thoughts as they arise. It is an all-encompassing attitude of mind, one that does not attempt to modify thoughts and feelings. With the absence of judgmental distinctions, the conditioned states are "clear and undisguised." The simple act of observation, devoid of analysis, is the dawning of the universal mind. Inevitably, practitioners inquire of themselves, their peers, and their teachers, "How can posing the observational question of "what is going on here?" by itself bring about meaningful change?" The answer is that consistent and diligent application of the observational mind of not-thinking liberates thinking from self-imposed bondage. Being able to consciously articulate what is going on, and to cultivate the new perspective of the mind stream—one that trusts the intuitive information that arises from contact with the previously unknown universal mind—begins the process of freeing oneself from the afflictive effects of conditioned states. Without application of habitual modes of preference making, thinking and not-thinking, once experienced as opposites, are now experienced as a complementary pair capable of acting in a beneficent harmony. This harmony is nonthinking itself, and is the natural result of observing thinking. The terms nonduality and nonthinking express the same unified experience and can be understood as synonyms.

Understanding the complementary nature of the relationship of dualistic pairs has wide-ranging effects. Replacing the perspective of "opposites" with "complementary" when dealing with dualistic pairs is not an abstract concept. It burrows into the intimate fabric of everyday relationships. For example, one issue that consistently comes up in the Zen study of lay practitioners is the perceived conflict between the demands of family life and career with the time for dedication to zazen. I have often heard people say, "I don't have time for my practice." This view encapsulates an incomplete understanding of how the dualistic pair of the mundane (daily life) and the sacred (zazen) interacts. Recognizing them as complements brings the Formal Mind and the unity of nonthinking directly into such activities as making supper, playing with one's children, creating a spreadsheet, and watching the moon set with your significant other. The unifying practice of zazen itself, however brief it may be, contains and supports the hopes, dreams, loves, anxieties, and confusion that all practitioners encounter. A young Vipassana teacher, who was also an extremely time-stressed resident MD, once related how she vowed to assume the sitting posture every day, if only for a minute. It's not how long we sit, but how we manifest the unanimity of nonthinking.

Triad 2P – Personal
Inquiry
Morality

Relating
The Key Question of Dualistic Interplay

"[T]he interface of delusion and enlightenment in their dynamic, nondual unity is extremely complex, elusive, and ambiguous."[29]

Hee-Jin Kim

Right Speech: Articulating words and phrases that penetrate, clarify, and liberate thought.

Right Action: Cultivating nonduality of mind makes needs of others central.

Right Livelihood: Noticing how closeness manifests when the path to nonduality is established.

Triad 2P: Relating

The key to understanding Relating is the study of dualities and their interplay. In Impartiality, we encountered two sets of dualistic pairs: Dogen's duality of thinking and not-thinking, and the question of how the sacred and mundane interact. In the quote above Professor Kim points out the inherent difficulties of the correlation of the pair of delusion and enlightenment. Actually, all dualities are problematic, some more than others.

Dualistic pairs are often considered opposites that need action to be merged, or to suppress the "harmful" side. Kim refers to the activity of the dualistic elements as "foci." He does so to emphasize that the elements act innately as complements. They are not oppositional elements to be blended into harmony with practice that would remove all negative effects of dualistic thinking. This simplistic view of how dualistic pairs relate obstructs how we deal with the reality of a situation. Furthermore, attempting to minimize the creative tension that exists between the pairs prevents the recognition of that same tension as the key to the process of liberation.

In Impartiality, one comes to understand that observation is the means of gaining knowledge of the tension of the dualistic pair of thinking and not-thinking. The observational method works universally in acquiring specific knowledge of the interplay of specific foci. The meditative study requires time, effort, and proper direction to clarify the characteristics of their complex association. The example below illustrates how Zen directly deals with dualities and their multifaceted interplay.

In Western philosophy, what constitutes the relationship between the mind and body has been a taxing problem since philosophy's inception, and it continues today. Thinkers have grappled with this thorny issue with no accepted conclusion. Carl Jung claimed the answer to the mystery was in the psyche; his patient,

Unfolding of the Eightfold Path

the physics Nobel laureate, Wolfgang Pauli, asserted the material world held the answer to the enigma. Even gifted intellectuals who were in a long, intimate association could not agree on where the truth lies. The nature of the interplay escaped them.

My first Zen teacher taught how to study and recognize this interplay without ever mentioning anything about dualistic pairs, interplay, or anything akin to those terms. Instead he used the dualistic pair of the mind-body relationship to provide the experiential understanding. His simple (but not easy) instructions were to sit upright in the precise zazen posture, breathe deeply, and stay awake to thoughts, feelings, sensations, and anything else that arose within consciousness. It soon became apparent to anyone who attempted this that a slumping body resulted in an unaware mind, and a fading awareness caused the body to lose its precision. Reconfiguring the posture refreshed the mind; renewing efforts at awareness straightened the posture. Failing and starting over again and again taught two important points.

1. The foci of the mind and body are complementary components acting in harmony to create the inclusive wholeness of nonduality.

2. The mind of nonduality does not transcend dualistic pairs. Rather nonduality is the complementary sum of the mind-body pair.

Discovering in oneself the essential features of the dualistic interplay opens the door to creative practice. Clarity and confidence replace confusion and apprehension. Applying the knowledge of the interplay in everyday encounters opens up mental space for self and others, undermining the walled-off existence perpetuated by taking dualistic pairs as opposites. Self and other are realized as another complementary pair.

At some point close to the beginning of my Zen practice, I began to drop my oppositional response to my teacher's instruction. I felt closer to him and his life. I began to notice how this changed our everyday encounters. We continued to meet with problems and misunderstandings, but a respectful dignity rooted in our common effort became the place where our energies and feelings converged. We remained distinct, yet the experience of oneness polished the sharp edges, leaving space for increased mutual caring. This growth in relationship altered my nascent understanding of nonduality in relationships from an abstraction to a visceral life-changing event. The power of Buddhist teaching resides in this very point: the middle path offers the creative way for the so-called opposites to recognize their inherent nondual relationship, and in so doing, transform themselves and the world around them as well.

Triad 2U – Universal
Inquiry
Wisdom

Introspection
Forms of the Natural Koan

"Prajna depends on both intellectual understanding and good intentions."[30]

Master Hsing Yun

Right View: Realizing that what is searched for, and what satisfies that search, is within the Mind.

Right Thought: Acquiring knowledge of the Natural Koan and forming intentions based on that knowledge.

Triad 2U: Introspection

Prior to our establishing a zazen practice, whatever we feel at any given moment dominates our mental landscape and is taken to be real and substantial. When we act in the world based on this incomplete view the result is almost always an inappropriate response. The conscious work at the heart of Zen sets the stage for the resolution of conditioned states. It begins with the realization that what was considered enduring and permanent lacks a persisting fixed self-nature. Impermanence is experienced when we observe the arising and continuous flow through our awareness of mental, emotional, and physical events. Phenomena are witnessed as ever-changing forms conditioned by previous events. This process is known as "just sitting" or silent illumination.

If one is capable of a white-hot awareness within zazen, conditioned states melt away over time. Most of us need extra help; we are unable to generate the necessary strength of concentration. Zen teachers of old recognized the needs of their students and devised many skillful means to aid them. Koan introspection is the one most avidly employed. In this practice, the key phrases of a case study are investigated, yielding a cognitive understanding of the point of the koan. Some teachers encourage delving more deeply in order to uncover subtler points.

Another introspective path available to practitioners considers and closely examines conditioned states as the forms of one's innate idiosyncratic Natural Koan.

Every individual manifests his or her Natural Koan in the form of a fundamental misperception, one that views the world with a mind of alienation and discontentment. It is intrinsic to human experience and precisely what obstructs our inherent potential for awakening. It arises out of the unique circumstances of an individual's life; hence its resolution must also be unique. The Natural Koan lies at the core of our suffering; resolving it is liberation.

Unfolding of the Eightfold Path

The word "natural" in Natural Koan implies ordinary or usual, and of nature, which is to say not wrong, not inadequate, just a naturally arising event. A koan is a question not answerable by usual means. Conceptual understanding does not resolve the question. Therefore, to resolve one's Natural Koan—the koan realized in life—Zen suggests application of the medicinal of Questioning.

Questioning deals with inquiring as to what is going on in the immediate moment. It is the passive mode of right concentration, an unremitting dwelling in the moment. Introspection probes the details of the moment, exploring the makeup of conditioned states, what triggers them, how they were formed, and their possible resolution. It is the dynamic mode of right concentration, intimately engaging with and understanding the forms of the Natural Koan.

Overemphasis of the passive side can result in our becoming satisfied with the pleasant sensations that may arise in zazen and slipping into a quiet sleepy state. Adding the more conscious and active movement of Introspection balances tranquility with the insight of discerning wisdom. The right thought of Introspection fosters a penetrating discrimination. "Gone is the fascination with the endless absorption in the undifferentiated."[31]

Introspection is the third aspect of the wisdom of awareness, the other two being study and the observing awareness of silent illumination. Adherence to its principles provides a thoroughgoing experiential knowledge of the substance and functioning of our mental and emotional processes. Without Introspection, our assumptions about the nature of self often remain deeply entrenched. We are born and are anesthetized to the true nature of the world around us by the gradual unfolding of our consciousness as we grow from baby to child to adult. A numbing familiarity prevents an authentic view of reality. We are like a person in a dark

Triad 2U: Introspection

room struggling to find a way out. Introspection cuts through the familiarity and little by little lifts the veil of the Natural Koan.

The discerning wisdom of Introspection also leads us to understand that the heart of the universe is intention. Knowing this changes the manner of how our intentions form and the quality of consciousness. We begin to understand that awareness free from the conditioned states' afflictive reactive responses opens us to making compassionate intentions. Good intentions yield good results. One's liberated speech, conduct, and caring for sentient beings readily overcome hindrances to respectful relations. Good intentions lead us to experience the world as a shared ownership, where each and every being has equal standing.

Triad 2U – Universal
Inquiry
Meditation

Insight
Receptivity

*"Amidst the high peaks a forlorn ape cries down to the moon.
The recluse chants while half the night a candle burns.
Who comprehends the place and time?
At a place deep within white clouds, a Zen monk sits."*[32]

Zen Master Yongming

Right Effort: Learning how to use the mundane as an integral part of practice.

Right Concentration: Learning to trust the unity of inquiry and response.

Right Mindfulness: Carrying the source of insight into the world.

Triad 2U: Insight

Master Yongming's observation, "deep within white clouds, a Zen monk sits," indicates that spiritual insight is discovered hidden within the human heart. The two attributes of right concentration—tranquility and insight—are cultivated in zazen, and then brought into the everyday world through the practice of right mindfulness. Tranquility separates the self from identification with the entities of the mind, allowing insight to arise within the sphere of consciousness. Insight is the product of a mind trained to observe itself, to be aware of its own activities and contents. Tranquility is holding still, the universe within the cosmic mudra; insight is accepting the truth of the nonfabricated voice of nature.

Tung-shan Liang-chieh describes the action of this voice:

> "Subtly included within the true, Inquiry and response come up together."[33]

Within the "true," conscious inquiry becomes a liberating force because of its identity with the meaningful "response." Question and answer are not serial events. They are two entangled, inseparable activities.

In Questioning, zazen practice moved beyond identification with thought and past conceptual problems to uncover the pathway leading to the unity of inquiry and response. The usual method of problem solving uses thought to think about something with hopes of deriving a course of action. Anxious striving for resolutions accompanies this process. In inquiry-response, thought and anxiety are put aside. An inquiry is made within the concentration of Informal Mind. In the non-serial way of inquiry-response, the response becomes conscious. Tung-shan Liang-chieh's way relies on a trust that comes about after all other paths are tried and found wanting.

Unfolding of the Eightfold Path

The upright posture of zazen gives us the preeminent opportunity to witness inquiry-response. Within the tranquility and insight of right concentration, one of the central points of Buddhist inquiry – the question of birth and death – naturally arises. Dogen advises to "Thoroughly investigate life in order to study death. Letting go and taking hold of life and death depend on refinement."[34] Refinement proceeds from direct experience. Reflections, thought, and especially, other's opinions on the matter yield nothing that is ultimately worthwhile in resolving the question of life and death.

A contemporary practitioner was asked, "What happens after we die?" She answered, "I don't know. I'm not dead yet." To consider birth and death requires a concrete reality to be meaningful; one must have the experience of dying to grasp it, not just a thought about it. In zazen, the unity of inquiry and the immediate response provides a manageable way of approaching this type of question. This is where the process of birth and death can be directly studied.

Birth and death can be looked at experientially within one lifetime in three ways: from conception until the last breath, within one thought, or during one breath cycle. Studying birth and death in a breath cycle is most meaningful because it lies within normal human perception. The other two, from conception to last breath and within one thought, tend toward abstractions because the time involved is either too long or too short. However, the breath cycle can be observed directly.

The most important detail of breathing during zazen is to allow each breath to be natural and smooth without interference. This allows one to be aware of the time between the end of one breath and the beginning of the next. Observing the breath being fully exhaled opens a large inner space, and invites enhanced attention. By not forcing anything, the beginning of the next breath happens of its own accord, and the time between the end and the beginning of the breaths gradually lengthens. The end of the breath cycle can be viewed as a physical death, a letting go, and an opening to vastness. Living within the time between breaths, one simply waits for the cycle to begin again, not knowing when it will occur. When the new breath arrives, it revivifies the body and mind, being new birth to both the physical and mental realms. Creating a continuity of awareness, one can become intimately familiar with the particulars of this process.

In Impartiality, right effort sets mundane concerns aside at the beginning of a sitting period and allows the mind to gain a measure of stability. In Insight, however, right effort brings the mundane back into practice as an integral part of the mental landscape, including all its confusion and conflicts. Confronting the issues (the forms of the Natural Koan) requires courage and a mature perspective. Zazen practice, especially at the start when one has minimal experience, can expose problems that appear to have no possible resolution. Hope seems dim or absent altogether. How can one stop a speeding train?

Our evening zazen sessions end with the practitioners reciting Dogen's Fukanzazengi. One time, after a few new people joined the group, the recitation became choppy and discordant. The mismatched speed, volume, and tone resulted in a mild cacophony. Even after a number of sessions the discord did not abate. The zazen leader advised the group members that chanting has listening at its heart. Each person must listen and meld their voice with each other. After this suggestion was made the disharmony disappeared. It was replaced by strong concurrent reading. It can be said the individuals are now making an instantaneous inquiry, "Am I in sync?" and if necessary make an immediate concordant response. Of course this is not done on the conceptual level. Inquiry-response resides "deep within white clouds" and is a natural outcome of a kindred alliance with the nonfabricated voice.

Triad 2U – Universal
Inquiry
Morality

Interconnection
Nature of Unity with All Beings

*"This moment contains ten thousand eons. It is past; it is future; it is present—all at once.
And it arrives as it leaves simultaneously."*[35]

John Daido Loori

*"'I am protecting the rain forest' develops to 'I am part of the rain forest protecting myself.
I am part of the rain forest recently emerged into thinking'"*[36]

John Seed

Right Speech: Connecting speech with insight.

Right Action: Connecting actions with insight.

Right Livelihood: Allowing the openness of Emptiness to express itself as connection with others.

Triad 2U: Interconnection

Dogen insisted on defining zazen as practice/realization, affirming his understanding that zazen is not meditation. Rather "it is the manifestation of ultimate reality."[37] This teaching is one of radical nonduality, that ultimate reality (thusness) expresses itself as Master Loori says "all at once." Meditators often look for some gain, seeking such outcomes as a calm demeanor, physical and psychological well-being, mental acuity, and greater awareness of human spirituality. The practitioner looks for the opportunity to enhance the sense of self. These changes strengthen character, opening the way for harmonious development of the intellect, emotions, and physical health of an individual. They see a lack, a deficiency, and work to relieve the gap between this perceived lack and the ideal.

Practice/realization does not create preferences for gaining any particular state of mind, nor does it try to disengage from unpleasant ones. The contents of the mind exist within a limitless mentality, with no desire for any specific experience. "All at once" denies there ever was a gap. Radical nonduality is not dependent on some special circumstance. It is available to all because it is everything at all times. If understood correctly it is the basis for a universal system of appropriate conduct. This understanding accurately defines Interconnection.

Western science may be on the threshold of grasping a new worldview. Historically, science has used analysis of events and beings as a means to successfully increase knowledge of the physical laws governing the universe. Delving into the subatomic level of matter, science now confronts the Eastern principle of interdependence and a holistic non-local universe: nothing exists by and of itself. Individual existence is always interrelated wherein if one thing changes, everything is immediately affected.

India, the historical hotbed of religion and philosophy, produced the remarkable image of Indra's Net that depicts interdependence and non-locality.

Unfolding of the Eightfold Path

> Far away in the heavenly abode of the great god Indra, there is a wonderful net that has been hung by some cunning artificer in such a manner that it stretches out infinitely in all directions. In accordance with the extravagant tastes of the deities, the artificer has hung a single glittering jewel in each eye of the net, and since the net itself is infinite in all dimensions, the jewels are infinite in number. There hang the jewels, glittering like stars of the first magnitude, a wonderful sight to behold. If we arbitrarily select one of the jewels for inspection and look closely at it, we will discover that in its polished surface there are reflected all the other jewels in the net, infinite in number. Not only that, but each of the jewels reflected in this one jewel is also reflecting all the other jewels, so that there is an infinite reflecting process occurring.[38]

Western thought confronts several elements of Indra's Net that are at odds with its philosophical tradition. First, the universe is infinite in dimension, an unimaginable feature. Second, it is nonhierarchical, having no identifiable center. While both concepts of universal structure are not unknown in the West, they have not enjoyed wide currency. Pascal's description of the universe is one of many that come close to conveying the idea of Indra's Net: "The universe is a sphere with an infinite circumference with the center at every point."

Third, a purpose for the universe cannot be pinpointed. With no theory of beginning or end the need for a divine creator drops away. Ludwig Wittgenstein may have had the universe's non-teleological makeup in mind when he proclaimed, "Not

Triad 2U: Interconnection

how the world is, but that it is, is the mystery." We continuously propagate new, never-ending impressions of how and what, but when ultimately "that" comes up all conjecture abates and is replaced with awe-filled silence.

The emotive realm of Indra's Net displays itself in Zen practice as a living reality. Joy and delight with another's company arise in daily zazen, but longer sessions attest to the intensity of intimacy that grows up among the practitioners. This is especially true of ango (practice period) attendees. One time, upon the completion of an ango, three carloads of participants were driving home on the same highway. Every 30 to 45 minutes they stopped for no other reason than to be with one another. They had became so close during the preceding months that they desired to be in each other's company. They had grown to love in a deep and abiding way, becoming polished reflecting jewels of Indra's Net expressing their mutual joy.

In the end, Sangha is a place of refuge where we intimately connect with our open and welcoming hearts. Imaginative sharing in the form of courteous speech and dignified conduct generously flows. The issue is no longer what we need for wholeness, but what we can provide to make other's lives happy and complete.

Section 3
Cultivating Psychological Well-being
Introduction to Triads 3P and 3U

*"Psychology can help develop a healthy sense
of self-structure.
Dharma eventually has us realize that our dualistic sense of self
and other is an illusion.
However, in order to really progress on the path, we need
confidence, trust, faith and courage."*

Lama Paldren Drolma

Triads 3P and 3U, Cultivating Psychological Well-being, represent the phase of practice during which practitioners obtain and develop a solid foundation on which thought, methods, inquiry, and insights are supported.

The practice of Buddhism requires psychological well-being so that insights into the nature of Buddhist teachings can be fully lived. This means that the implications of an insight must be deeply understood and fully integrated into the thoughts and actions in daily life.

Unfolding of the Eightfold Path

Triad 3P consists of learning the personal, intrapersonal, and interpersonal orientations that are the essentials for a well-adapted life and for taking on the rigors of Zen practice. Understanding and implementing the personal, intrapersonal, and interpersonal orientations establishes the necessary solid "self structure" of psychological well-being

Triad 3U goes beyond just understanding what the orientations are. Cultivating stability, acceptance, and worthiness leads one to being able to perceive and live the unity of the psychological and spiritual aspects of our nature. Breakthrough moments require a firm basis of emotional well-being. Without integration, insights remain naïve experiences that lack the depth and maturity that supports true transformation.

Triad 3P – Personal
Psychological Well-being
Wisdom

Personal Orientation
Basis of Practice

The way through the world is more difficult to find than the way beyond it.

Wallace Stevens

"The madness, of course, for each of us will have to be sorted out."[39]

Alice Walker

Right View: Understanding the form and timing of the work required for spiritual practice. Engaging with the self with utmost dignity, understanding the nature of roles and rules.

Right Thought: Nurturing a balanced focus toward life that understands the danger of trying to solve problems through spiritual gain.

Triad 3P: Personal Orientation

Before we establish a spiritual practice, we must first construct a foundation that is built on living a full and complete life. When we embark upon a spiritual quest, we add this responsibility to the many others already in place in our lives. John Welwood, in his book *Toward a Psychology of Awakening*, examines how people who seek awakening sometimes attempt to sidestep the difficulties of worldly life by assuming spiritual insight will solve all their problems. Welwood calls this misguided effort "spiritual bypassing."[40] It is a common but mistaken response to the discomfort and dissatisfaction of daily life.

In spiritual bypassing, problematic emotional and personal issues are left unresolved, while spiritual practices are emphasized as a way to find release from the pain associated with them. Spirituality becomes the focus through which life is judged, giving it specialness out of proportion with the fundamental needs of the individual. Trying to forge ahead without answering both our personal and spiritual needs leads to developmental disharmony. Ultimately, we cannot avoid addressing unresolved concerns; if the imbalances are not dealt with directly, they will come in the back door, usually in chaotic and destructive forms.

Spiritual bypassing exacerbates already existing imbalances such as emotional distress, desire for the unattainable, anger and defensiveness, insecurity and its counterpart arrogance, various anxieties, low self-esteem, and self-hatred. We avoid spiritual bypassing when we fulfill all of the responsibilities life brings without evasion. Facing everything directly does not mean the imbalances will be settled, but in doing so, there is at least a chance for positive change. Avoidance is the start of the detour that only leads back to the beginning with no actual beneficial change occurring in our lives.

Personal Orientation is the opposite of spiritual bypassing. It recognizes and accepts duties as they come without shirking

Unfolding of the Eightfold Path

responsibility. It cooperates with the developmental process of maturity. Deliberate steadfast actions and an uncompromising introspection are the chief qualities of a correct orientation. Personal Orientation does not try to evade the everyday problems by assuming spiritual growth will alleviate their effects.

One way we encourage spiritual bypassing is by misunderstanding the nature and place of roles and rules. In our daily life, the roles we take on and the rules of social engagement are powerful and sometimes insidious forces. They often overwhelm our view of them as only tentatively agreed upon relationships invented so that we can get on with the business of living. When we mistakenly view the roles and rules as fixed and inflexible, our inner observational vantage point is lost. The "for yourself" teaching of the Buddha is nowhere to be found. Illegitimate authority is granted where it should not be given. No teacher, parent, employer, spouse, or anyone else has the ability to comprehend accurately one's ultimate path in life. Keeping in mind we are always responsible for everything we think, say, and do, Buddha's teaching on Spiritual Autonomy maintains a clear focus on the actual nature of societal, cultural, and religious roles and rules.

Recently I heard a story that illustrates how a Zen practitioner remained true to herself in the face of a great deal of outside pressure to turn away from the right view and right thought of Personal Orientation. This woman, let's call her Martha, became interested in Zen and was introduced to a famous, charismatic teacher by a friend. Martha was initially attracted by the teacher's manner of expression and his place within the Buddhist community. She practiced with him for several years, but she was not completely satisfied with the outcome of her practice. She was taught that Zen had the answers to all her problems, mundane or sacred. However, not much attention was given to the personal side of practice, and many issues remained festering despite her best efforts. Her friend, by now a priesthood candidate, made little of Martha's concerns, consistently pointing out the fame of the temple and teacher, as if this could help resolve Martha's problems.

Later Martha and her friend attended a sesshin at another center in the area, where Martha met a teacher with whom she in due course formed a long-term relationship. When she declared her attraction to the sesshin leader's inclusive approach to practice, Martha's friend criticized the new teacher's commonplace appearance and teaching style, negatively comparing them with their present teacher's charismatic expertise in guiding students. Later, others in their Sangha discouraged Martha's interest in the other priest. After a reflective period, Martha eventually trusted her inner wisdom, joined the new priest's organization, and subsequently enjoyed many years of pleasant and fruitful practice. Once, she heard her new teacher remark about himself, "Nobody wants an ordinary guy as their Zen teacher." Martha found the opposite to be true. She found in the new Sangha the means and support to come to grips simultaneously and creatively with personal concerns and spiritual endeavor. If she had given over to the unwise counsel of her friend, she may have continued to feel frustrated in her attempts to creatively address her personal problems.

Unfortunately, there are many examples of Zen teachers and practitioners who consider spiritual insight alone sufficient for a balanced and happy life. You can recognize them by the unnecessary difficulties they impose on their students. The personal and universal are equally legitimate concerns and practice must contain the means of resolution for both. Sometimes it is the "ordinary guy" whose evenhanded wisdom provides the clear direction for us to make our ". . . way through the world."

Triad 3P – Personal
Psychological Well-being
Meditation

Intrapersonal Orientation
Progress

Sing in me, Muse, and through me tell the story.

Homer

Right Effort: Recognizing achievement and change and using that knowledge to overcome resistance to practice.

Right Concentration: Cultivating lighthearted pleasure and contentment within the Informal Mind.

Right Mindfulness: Establishing satisfaction and an attitude of delight as a fact of life within Informal Posture.

Triad 3P: Intrapersonal Orientation

Intrapersonal Orientation confirms the role zazen has in one's life. In this phase of practice the skills of observation and introspection develop and become our constant orientation of attention in zazen. The wide expanse afforded the Informal Mind provides room for all mental phenomena, letting the Muse have her way. Our personal story has the freedom to exist without any desire to suppress or control the process in any way.

Intrapersonal Orientation also creates a space where we can note progress and its stabilizing effects. This minimizes the modulations of effort that are caused by inexperience, poor discipline, and false enthusiasm. Intrapersonal Orientation honestly reflects on our achievements or the lack of them. There is no codification of how to tread the path. Students of Zen since the beginning have had to struggle with the unknown in zazen. Teachers stand by and watch with attentiveness, help where they can, but tend not to interfere. They know direct experience can only be encouraged, not shared.

The contemporary teacher mentioned earlier taught his students how to gauge the effectiveness of their progress in practice. He instructed beginners to practice for six months, reflect on the changes that occurred during that time, commit to memory the positive results, and then, when the will to practice inevitably wanes, recollect the changes to foster a revitalized effort. Every Zen practitioner will eventually face within themselves a resistance to practice. This resistance comes in many forms and can subtly undermine a consistent and appropriate application of will. Keeping previously recognized achievements in mind helps to diminish the negative effects of resistance.

The following story exemplifies the beneficial effects of resolving resistance. A new Zen practitioner named Elizabeth, shortly after the start of a month-long practice period, asked about oryoki,

Unfolding of the Eightfold Path

the formal way of eating meals. She was puzzled and troubled by its formality and defined manner. Meals were an ordeal for her because she thought the traditional Zen way was outmoded and obtuse. After listening to the description of her discomfort, the practice director advised her to temporarily drop her opinion, attempt to approach oryoki meals with an open mind, and to come back to her if she could not accomplish the change of perspective.

The month passed without Elizabeth expressing further concerns about the meals. During the check-out time, the practice director asked Elizabeth about her ensuing oryoki experience. She related that dropping her initial opinion offered her an opportunity to enter into the serving, eating, cleaning, and chanting with less resistance. As time went on, affection for the practical wisdom embedded in oryoki practice spontaneously arose and replaced the residual criticism. By the end of the training, Elizabeth declared that the shared experience of oryoki was for her like falling in love. She shared the experience of many other zazen practitioners who learn how to appreciate the holistic nature of the many forms of practice. Effort in practice creates joy and understanding.

Walking meditation is another good example of how we can transform a seeming disruption into an aid to awakening. Sitting in zazen enhances continuity of awareness. When we rise and immediately begin to walk the transition is smooth and the zazen attitude is maintained. With practice we become skilled at transferring the continuity of awareness from immobile sitting to animating the movements of the Informal Posture of walking. Adding the slow steps of walking with the established coordination of breathing clarifies how the concentration of the Informal Mind can be successfully channeled into mindful movement. When we are able to skillfully complete this transition we can move with ease and dexterity. Other practices such as chanting and bowing are much the same, and they invite us to instill them with the same attentiveness. In this way coherence becomes the norm of experience.

Triad 3P: Intrapersonal Orientation

One other important aspect of Intrapersonal Orientation is how it informs our understanding of the dualistic pair of tranquility and insight. Taken together they make up the Informal Mind of right concentration.

The dynamic awareness of tranquility relates intimately with our ever-changing mental landscape. We embody its effects as a profound sense of well-being. Insight is wisdom and clarity of vision that arises spontaneously within the sphere of tranquility.

Learning how tranquility and insight interact requires a penetrating awareness because of the exceptionally subtle and indefinite territory where they link. Unwinding the situation is not at all hopeless; a marvelous opportunity presents itself to us within the uncertainty.

To overcome the inherent ambiguity, we must avoid the extremes of being satisfied with the pleasant feelings that arise in tranquility and an overbearing striving to attain insight. Both of these attitudes miss the point. In order to maintain balance and allot both tranquility and insight equal significance, one must maintain the basic attributes of the Informal Mind:

- Witnessing thoughts and feelings without "turning away or touching"
- Sustaining a diligent effort
- Returning over and over again to the continuity of awareness after losing and regaining the thread of attention

Progress in meditation practice results from long-standing efforts; difficulties abound and no shortcuts are possible. Yet we must value and enjoy any degree of peace, joy, and contentment that arises within our conscientious endeavors.

Triad 3P – Personal
Psychological Well-being
Morality

Interpersonal Orientation
Accomplishment

*"In the heart of the night,
The moonlight framing
A small boat drifting,
Tossed not by the waves
Nor swayed by the breeze."*[41]

Zen Master Dogen

Right Speech: Experiencing satisfaction with simple controlled discourse.

Right Action: Practicing restraint in conduct mirrors the Formal Mind.

Right Livelihood: Responding to the world's needs with a sense of personal responsibility. Trying to find the edge of what we consider "our life."

Triad 3P: Interpersonal Orientation

Within continuity of awareness, we become able to genuinely perceive the emphasis of Zen's teaching on impermanence. Continuity of awareness is exactly living in attentive accord with the unfolding universe just as it is without interjecting analysis or opinion. Dogen's assessment of transience in the Fukanzazengi—"...besides form and substance are like the dew on the grass, emptied in an instant, vanished in a flash"[42]—accurately characterizes the fleeting nature of phenomena. Aspiration for awakening and transformation of the self occur at the core of the experience of impermanence. Impermanence teaches us that "Tossed not by the waves nor swayed by the breeze" describes a skillful orientation within interpersonal relationships. When we remove the karmic obstructions to free-flowing movement, we can work creatively in our spiritual, social, and intellectual lives. Then, even if a formed intention proves to be as fragile as a "small boat drifting" the waves and breeze will not hinder our steadfast practice.

Buddhism is essentially a teaching of relationships. It promotes a pragmatic approach. Hindrances, such as negative emotions, give way so that we can benefit from happy and mutually beneficial social interactions. Inter-personal Orientation allows us to keep impermanence at the forefront, knowing it is not an obstacle for change, but a channel to awakened behavior. When we understand life situations to be fluid and flexible, then even the most trying of circumstances can be transformed into something beneficial.

Imagine that you are vehemently criticized by another person, which arouses anger. If you outwardly express the anger in an attempt to get even for the criticism, the exchange may deteriorate into a feud and bring about hard feelings for both parties. However, if you closely notice the anger as it arises and choose

Unfolding of the Eightfold Path

not to express it, then you have an opportunity for an exceedingly creative response that may soothe the other person's harsh feelings. Even if it does not help in that way, opting to not respond with anger ensures that your continuity of awareness is not damaged; in fact it may actually increase in strength. When we avoid expressing negative emotions, it allows them to be transformed from harmful energy into beneficial energy. Mindfully embodying our emotions—positive and negative—establishes restraint and increases the sense of personal responsibility for ourselves, for those with whom we are in immediate contact, and eventually for the world at large.

Interpersonal Orientation also requires us to answer the questions: "Where is the edge of my life?" "Where does my personal responsibility end and others' begin?" "What is mine, and what belongs to others?" The concept of private property is well-defined in our society, but ownership of items of common use leads into gray areas. A Dharma friend of mine named John related a story about one encounter he had that caused him to consider the issue of personal and universal ownership.

John was on his way to an out-of-town sesshin. In an airport restroom he entered a stall and found it strewn with paper. He turned back the urge to move to another, and took the time to clean up before leaving.

Later during dokusan, he asked the teacher his view on the first Bodhisattva vow of "Sentient Beings are numberless, I vow to save them." John said he often asked this because he was confused about it. The teacher's reply surprised him, "It's not complicated. When you are using a public toilet, you own it. No matter what the condition or how you came to it, while you are there, it is your responsibility. And so it is with everything else that comes to you. Each thought, sensation, will to action, human or animal encounter, you own it. When you own it you are serving all life."

Triad 3U – Universal
Psychological Well-being
Wisdom

Psychological Maturity
Stability

*"The Sage taught the entire system for the sake
of wisdom.
Therefore, with the desire to ward off suffering, one should develop
wisdom."*[43]

Shantideva

Right View: Witnessing the hand-in-glove activities of the so-called internal and external worlds of human experience.

Right Thought: Relying on the Buddha's teaching of Dependent Origination.

Triad 3U: Psychological Maturity

Our discussion of Personal Orientation introduced spiritual bypassing: the misguided attempt to resolve everyday problems through spiritual insight only. When we achieve a state of Psychological Maturity we learn to avoid the dangerous practice of spiritual bypassing and replace it with personal responsibility and wholehearted participation in the maturation process. Personal Orientation enables the practitioner to develop a stable practice; Psychological Maturity exhibits stable practice in everyday life.

Beginners to Zen practice soon realize how conditioned states operate in our lives. Our first understanding often takes the form of "I am the problem," a perspective that personalizes the conditioned state and its effects. This false deduction arises from our Western view that human nature is innately flawed. Zazen practice develops the skills of observation and questioning so that we can restate the issue as "I have a problem." This view is a more accurate assessment of our relationship to conditioned states and allows us to formulate an attitude of mind beyond recrimination and self-blame. We, of course, are responsible for working with our conditioned states, but attaching blame to others or ourselves for their existence is an unhelpful perspective and hinders our attempts to resolve them.

When we are able to understand spiritual bypassing, we can close the gap between the psychological (personal) and spiritual (universal). If we maintain an equal regard for both functions, we establish a strong foundation from which to address our conditioned states. Understanding the truth of Buddha's teaching of Dependent Origination makes this possible.

The Lankatavara Sutra defines Dependent Origination as, "Phenomena do not rise independently; they arise dependent on each other." Every person, event, thought, and action arise together

Unfolding of the Eightfold Path

from a set of causes and conditions. Dependent Origination teaches that unity is the norm, not separation, although we routinely think otherwise. Shantideva's advice to "develop wisdom" encourages us to see patterns of wholeness.

When looking at the tangled backside of a tapestry, the yarn appears chaotic and random. However, if one turns it over, the harmony of the artistry is revealed. When we consider the spiritual question along with the psychological it is like we are turning the tapestry over.[44] Our situation, whatever it is, demonstrates a perfect accord with the underlying circumstances. As a cloud is in perfect harmony with the wind that pushes it along, so too our unfolding life is synchronous with the environmental conditioning that makes up our physical and mental being.

The following stories recount two contrasting incidents, one illustrating the effects of spiritual bypassing (not witnessing the harmonious side of the tapestry), and the other of Psychological Maturity.

Some time ago, a ten-year student of Zen found the circumstances at her practice center untenable for a number of legitimate reasons. She informed her teacher that she was leaving. He responded with anger, derided her effort, stripped her of her priest robes, and set up all sorts of roadblocks to an amiable and constructive parting.

This unfortunate event contrasts with another parting of master-disciple. Here too the student realized he needed to leave. He and his teacher discussed the situation. The teacher was deeply disappointed as they had been together for a long time. However, he moved past his personal feelings, responding with understanding and helpful advice. The teacher's attitude assisted the student's transition, eventually aiding him to become a student of a new teacher.

Triad 3U: Psychological Maturity

The first teacher dominated and manipulated his student. He had the mistaken idea that he "owned" the student. The second teacher understood spiritual autonomy, and thus was capable of listening to and acknowledging the student's need. His understanding of spiritual relationships resulted in progress for his student.

The first student was victimized by resentment and blame, hounded by a person who had prematurely assumed the teacher role without resolving underlying personality issues. The second student enjoyed the benefit of a teacher who had developed strength of character. His teacher demonstrated a firmly established stable Psychological Maturity that shielded his student from injurious anger and bitterness.

Triad 3U – Universal
Psychological Well-being
Meditation

Embracing
Acceptance

This morning as I wake,
I vow with all beings,
To realize everything without exception
Embracing the ten directions.[45]

Right Effort: Finding energy and encouragement in a deepening understanding of the self.

Right Concentration: Practicing with poise and self-reliance, undeterred by the presence of conditioned states.

Right Mindfulness: Internalizing the negative effects of conditioned states.

Triad 3U: Embracing

In Triad 2P, we saw that the practice of Impartiality allows the universal mind of not-thinking to observe the impermanence of the mind, including problematic conditioned states. Observation increases our awareness of how conditioned states are triggered, but does little to resolve the afflictive emotions that accompany them. At this stage the newly dawned universal mind plays a minor role.

Later in our spiritual development we nurture the skill of Embracing and become able to see the "ten directions" just as they are. We observe the generation and passing of our thoughts and emotions without embellishment. Previously, "to realize without exception" was based on tolerance with its inherent judgmental component. Now our open-minded perspective of acceptance accommodates without judgment.

The conditioned states operate in us as before, except that the universal mind has grown to be a potent force. It surrounds them with inner kindness, cutting off their negative effects from manifesting in the world. When we practice Embracing, we internalize the conditioned states. This gives us the inner strength to stop their harmful effects from leaking into relationships. The inner kindness also intensifies our deep introspection of their form and function. Embracing strengthens coping strategies with a conditioned state, but does not dispel its root cause.

Another even more important consequence of the potent universal mind is to increase our capacity to hear the nonfabricated voice of Buddhanature with newfound clarity. When we can quiet the internal chatter connected with conditioned states, the voice can be clearly perceived.

The *Song of the Jewel Mirror Awareness* is Tung-shan Liang-Chieh's poem that describes the process required to attain and maintain the Jewel Mirror Awareness. In it, one of the verses explains the nature of the nonfabricated voice:

Unfolding of the Eightfold Path

> Although it is not fabricated,
> It is not without speech.
> It is like facing a jewel mirror:
> Form and image behold each other.[46]

It is not fabricated by human agency. It has no beginning or end. It also has the means to intimately communicate. When form and image behold each other, the Jewel Mirror insight of nonduality is the natural result. The nonfabricated voice of nonduality is the outcome of the correct relationship of dualistic pairs. It acts in us as a unified vision free of conflict.

Even though Zen practitioners make stringent efforts to find the path of nonduality, oftentimes obstructions such as persistent skepticism block understanding of the authenticity of the experience. Zen practice carried out in close association with others offers the opportunity for validating authentic experience. Within practice, close personal relationships erode barriers, and the Jewel Mirror is made real within the ordinary. It is not necessary to look far afield for examples of this type of vision; they are found within the simplicity of everyday life.

Back when Zen was just beginning to attract a large number of practitioners in the West, one Zen teacher hoped to remain familiar with all attendees of his temple. After morning service he would stand in a small alcove and bow in gassho to everyone individually as they filed out. I don't know how well that worked for him, but each time I stepped up and met him one-on-one, some of the doubt I had about what I was attempting dropped away. Later I had a five-year association with an elderly Japanese woman who was a lifelong Zen adherent. I would see her almost every day. When we met, she would greet me with a smile, a gassho, and a bow. Her unquestioning acceptance conveyed me beyond myself into her inescapable cheeriness.

Triad 3U: Embracing

The nonfabricated voice presents itself in intimate encounters, with encompassing feelings of wholeness. It is the voice wherein the Zen essential of trust is communicated and cultivated. Stabilizing this realization refines our inner kindness and develops confidence in practice.

Triad 3U – Universal
Psychological Well-being
Morality

Dignity
Worthiness

"Dignified manner is Buddha Dharma; decorum is the essential teaching."[47]

Zen Master Daigen Ikko Narasaki

Right Speech: Being aware of how trust and confidence manifest in tone and word choice.

Right Action: Being aware of how trust and confidence manifest in all manner of physical expressions.

Right Livelihood: Cultivating the insight that the whole world is ours. Trying to find the edge of what we consider "our responsibility."

Triad 3U: Dignity

In the quote above, Daigen Ikko Narasaki Roshi says a dignified manner *is* exactly the Buddha Dharma; he does not imply that it only expresses it. In his view, the movements and manner of Zen practitioners are one with the embodiment of the Buddha Dharma. He goes on to say, "Decorum is the essential teaching." The dictionary defines decorum as restraint, etiquette, modesty, and respectability. Narasaki Roshi would probably say that those attributes perform wonderful service in creating human courtesy, but that his decorum and dignity are rooted in inner kindness and awareness of the nonfabricated voice.

The term "awareness" in some places has taken on the meaning of standing apart and viewing dispassionately. Dignity does not stand on the sidelines; it penetrates daily activity and creates a wide acceptance for others to inhabit. It carries the comforting effects of inner kindness to the outer world.

In Zen practice when one desires to strike a bell "correctly" one must hit it at the incipient moment, with precise force, and with interconnection to the environment. The person and bell vanish, leaving the nonfabricated voice alone to wield the striker. Practitioners who are capable of this skill communicate the spirit of "dignified manner" to the Sangha. The nonfabricated voice's heart is dignity, and it has the ability to effect an emotional response in the listener. It is clearly present for those with eyes to see and ears to hear.

In 2000, a memorial service commemorating Dogen's birth in 1200 was held in Japan. Many Western Zen teachers and students participated in the ceremony. Afterwards, Japanese Zen teachers who had never practiced outside of Japan remarked about the noteworthy way of being that many of the Western teachers naturally possessed. They witnessed dignity in action and were

Unfolding of the Eightfold Path

impressed by the Western teachers' embodied dignity. Westerners demonstrated the fruit of their years of practice in decorum of speech and movement. Their Zen practice had dispelled the barriers to the penetration of inner kindness, freeing their minds and bodies to move with alacrity and unself-conscious grace.

John O'Donohue, in his book *Beauty: The Invisible Embrace*, conveys what the Japanese teachers witnessed in their Western progeny:

> Ultimately, reverence is respect for mystery.
> But it is more than an attitude of mind;
> It is also physical –
> A dignified attention of the body
> Showing the sacred is already here.[48]

The embrace of inner kindness flows beyond the confines of practitioners' lives, marking them with a unique dignity. Self-importance is tossed aside replaced with a sense of wonder and delight.

The ability to speak and move in a dignified manner is the ultimate outcome of psychological well-being. It is a quality that is rooted in earned worthiness, and it creates in us the ability to face life's challenges successfully. Zen is always practical; it is never an empty aesthetic. As practitioners we intimately grasp that dignity is the medicinal that relieves the distance between the Buddha Dharma and conduct in the world. Making it our own lights a beacon for others who labor for an understanding of kindness and harmony.

Section 4
Establishing the Awareness of the "Don't-Know Mind"
Introduction to Triads 4P and 4U

"Seeking the Way
Amid the deepest mountain path,
The retreat I find
None other than,
My primordial home: satori"[49]

Zen Master Dogen

Somewhere in the past, an unknown species of Homo became Homo sapiens through the discovery of the path to self-awareness.[50] With self-awareness, the heretofore naïve sense of oneness was replaced with a greatly enhanced discernment of time and relationships. These newly self-aware beings also gained a capability to realize their true nature through the embodiment of wisdom. However, because human beings possess only the capability of embodying wisdom, not the certainty, we stand in a transitional state, exiled from the naïve, but not yet fully entrenched in the world of the aware. Resolving this transient situation demands unusual effort and commitment. In Triads 4P and 4U, we move to the edge of the cliff of unknowing, accompanied by inconceivability and our ancestors' undaunted spirit of exploration.[50]

Triad 4P – Personal
Establishing 'Don't-Know Mind'
Wisdom

Inevitability
Recognition of the Human Condition

"The wind blows hard among the pines
Toward the beginning of an endless past.
Listen: you've heard everything."[51]

Shinkichi Takahashi

Right View: Witnessing events without elaboration.

Right Thought: Being face-to-face with the inconceivable: the unthinkable and implausible are always before us.

Triad 4P: Inevitability

We pass from childhood to adolescence to adulthood not knowing the answers to the big questions of our lives, trying to assemble understanding from shadowed evidence picked up along the way, meeting death head-on with only guesses and hopes as companions. There are times when clues coalesce into something more. Once a ten-year old boy offered his assessment of the human situation. In a science class one day, his mind opened to a vision where he saw that we are all passengers on the surface of a rock hurtling through the vast void of space. It was startling for him to wake up to this stark reality. He struggled for a while with unsettled thoughts and feelings.

In 1968 many bookstores in the city I was living in displayed a picture of the Earth taken by the Apollo 8 mission halfway to the moon. This photograph is common nowadays, but when it was first taken the view was as startling as the boy's insight. It aroused feelings of inconceivability, a kind of homecoming where beauty awakens wonder.

THE FULL EARTH

The Big Blue Marble shawled in white strands of impermanence.
Viewing her, our relationships come into question.
The home that generated our form,
The home of our brothers and sisters,
Of awe and mystery.
Alone in the vastness we may discover who we really are.[52]

Simultaneously with the photograph's distribution, the Vietnam War waged on. After one of the most horrific bombings, an elder

Unfolding of the Eightfold Path

spokesman of the San Francisco Zen Center rose up after a Dharma talk and asked Shunryu Suzuki Roshi, "What can we do about the bombing? What can we do about the war?" Vigorous loud protests were taking place all over the country. That night's attendees carried that spirit into the meditation hall. We expected a response equal to our sense of outrage. Suzuki Roshi acknowledged the importance of the question with a short moment of reflection before quietly answering, "Find the seeds of war in yourself."

The suggested action seemed all out of proportion with the problem. A few murmurs arose from the audience, but nothing much else was said. I left that night with a question that sparked many years of inner dialogue. The question of conflict and concord joined the file of many dualistic pairs that posed irresolvable paradoxes.

Years later, when the inner kindness of Embracing showed me the way to surround apparent contradictions, the study of the paradoxical relationships within Suzuki Roshi's challenging assertion began to make sense. I became familiar with two internal pathways in relating to conflict and concord:

1. With an act of will, one attains control over the urge to lash out in anger. Here the conflict is kept inside and outer violence avoided. Coping strategies are used to maintain restraint.

2. One observes the relationship of conflict and concord through the lens of thinking and not-thinking. Understanding the relationship of thinking and not-thinking as a complementary pair is nonthinking. Realizing nonthinking, the nondual experience of conflict and concord, liberates one from the urge to strike out. Conflict remains internalized, but in this case, coping is not needed. Coping is no longer necessary because nonduality resolves the root cause of violent impulses.

Triad 4P: Inevitability

Conflict in the human heart and in daily relations is inevitable, but violent behavior is not. It is the central attitude from which authentic practice develops. Buddha proclaimed this way of action in Dhammapada #5 where he teaches, "Never at any time in this world are hostilities resolved by hostility. But by kindness they are resolved. This is an eternal truth."

Triad 4P – Personal
Establishing 'Don't-Know Mind'
Meditation

Clarifying
Without Lack

My works are the issue of pure and single experience, who is the one true mistress.
These rules are sufficient to enable you to know the true from the false.

Leonardo da Vinci

Right Effort: Making a wholehearted attempt at plumbing the point of connection with impermanence.

Right Concentration: Relinquishing the anxiety of desire to have, to gain, and to do better. Exploring the boundaries of the Informal Mind freed from the limits that desire imposes.

Right Mindfulness: Cultivating satisfaction and an attitude of delight within the Informal Posture. Exploring the boundaries of the Informal Posture freed from the limits that desire imposes.

Triad 4P: Clarifying

"The gap between more and enough never closes," declares a Jimmy John sandwich shop wall poster. The saying perfectly describes the First and Second Noble Truths. "The gap" is dukkha, the root of why suffering arises. "More and enough never closes" describes desire, the cause of dukkha, and why it goes on and on. As long as there is a sense of lack—the pernicious sense that somehow we are not enough—real life is far away, with the disturbing influences of conditioned states crowding out clear thinking. The Zen prescription consists of repeated immersions in emptiness, the Third Noble Truth—the cessation of dukkha.

Emptiness is radical openness to the world, giving people, objects, and events the room to be just what they are. It is the clarity of mind that puts aside attempts to reorder reality to fill a sense of lack. All is lost as long as we believe that the cure lies in trying to satisfy ever-manifesting desires. However, doing away with the search itself closes the gap "between more and enough." It is resigning from the task of the never-ending grind of feeding the hungry ghosts. Just taking the medicine of emptiness seems simple enough, but uprooting a sense of lack requires clarity of vision.

Emptiness grows out of the analysis of the self into the five skandhas of form, feelings, perceptions, impulses, and consciousness. The skandhas are tentative and ephemeral: the body is never still, feelings come and go, perceptions are rapid and never ending, impulses arise from triggered memories, consciousness is like the surface of the wind-blown sea. Thus, a Buddhist experiences the self as a parade of ever-changing formations, without a discernible beginning or a predictable end. When asked we all agree that impermanence is the natural order of life. However, just knowing that does not grant us the ability to think and behave in accord with causes and conditions. Attachments are sticky and clarity is easily lost.

Unfolding of the Eightfold Path

When I was a young and a newly ordained priest, I lived at a small Zen center. One of my regular duties was setting up and monitoring the weekly schedule of zazen sessions.

One Thanksgiving, I arranged the meditation hall as usual for evening zazen: straightening the cushions, dusting the altar, and freshening the flowers and water. The night was dark and unsettled, with heavy rain at an inch an hour from an early winter storm. I stood by the door to welcome attendees, even though I had concluded that no one was going to come because of the holiday and weather conditions. The downpour reminded me of scenes in movies that portended a problematic occurrence. I began to feel maudlin and lonely. I reflected that everything would be better if I had a family to alleviate the loneliness, and an apartment with comforts beyond a small space with a rollaway bed. What had Zen done for me anyway? My self-pity took my mood lower and lower. No one came, but I waited past the normal starting time just in case of delay on the road. After fifteen minutes, I decided to sit down, hoping the sitting would drag me out of my funk.

As I smoothed my robes, I heard a shuffle on the stairs. I got up and greeted two old Zen friends whom I had not seen in some months. They had driven thirty miles on half-flooded freeways. They too had felt a few pangs of holiday-driven lonesomeness, and thought I might be in the same boat. We meditated together and afterwards shared a meal. That night, laughter and companionship cleared the air, driving out the ghosts, restoring clarity, and, at least for a while, relieving the gap between more and enough. Wall poster sayings are not always correct.

Triad 4P – Personal
Establishing 'Don't-Know Mind'
Morality

Integrating
Seamless Serving

"If your thoughts are not self-centered and do not interfere, your natural faculties and your Buddha-nature will exert themselves, and you will be able to do as you desire."[53]

Soyu Matsuoka Roshi

Right Speech: Speaking, like chanting, is done by listening.

Right Action: Acting, like walking meditation, is done with harmony of attention and body movements.

Right Livelihood: Recognizing and serving the needs of others to awaken.

Triad 4P: Integrating

Matsuoka Roshi asserted that when self-centered interests no longer dominate, our natural faculties will animate our behavior, for use as one wishes. Reading this quote one is drawn to inquire: What are our natural faculties?

In the anecdote included in the discussion of Interpersonal Orientation, the teacher at the sesshin John attended taught that all encounters afford the opportunity for ownership and service. Ownership is taking responsibility for whatever a relationship or circumstance requires; serving is practicing with a magnanimous mind without desire for recognition or reward.

Zen training roles offer the chance to study and penetrate the meaning of ownership and service. Both are central to fulfilling the role of Jisha (abbot's attendant). The Jisha trains to be alert to the abbot's surroundings in order to make sure everything goes smoothly for him in ceremonies, meals, and keeping the temple schedule. The Jisha submits his/her will to the role. They place oneness with the task over personal concerns. The Jisha's conscious submission of will leads to integrity of action, where duties are performed with a minimum of internal constraints. Matsuoka Roshi's "and you will do as you desire" is alive and in bloom.

In the early '90s, Hokyoji Zen Practice Center sponsored a sesshin led by a Zen teacher from a Japanese training monastery. He brought a number of disciples with him. One of them, apparently a senior monk, acted as the Ino, or practice director for the weekend. Before the start of the sesshin, he presented an orientation letting us know what to expect. He politely answered questions, and also spoke to our unstated concerns.

Once underway, I noticed that the Ino spent a good deal of his time walking slowly around the meditation hall, alert to the practitioners' needs. He straightened posture, assisted beginners at mealtime, and helped translate the teacher's instruction and talks. His watchfulness continued for the rest of the retreat. His dedication was remarkable in itself, but what was even more noteworthy was his goodwill and unfaltering patience.

At the end of the sesshin, a few of the attendees talked about the Ino and the effect he had on us. After a while we were able to summarize our thoughts and impressions. We all had experienced what we termed "correction" by some teachers. "Correction" communicated a judgmental attitude, inducing a bitter feeling in the one being corrected. We also had experienced "instruction" where the teacher communicated his message or lesson without criticism of any sort. Instead their deep regard and acceptance inspired the same in the one being instructed.

The Ino at the sesshin was of the latter variety, imparting "instruction" without pretense. His training had produced in him the compassion and wisdom practitioners seek. His "natural faculties" were on display without the hindrance of self-centeredness. He had made oneness his own and had freely given it away. He was and continues to be a model of what is possible in Zen practice.

Triad 4U – Universal
Establishing 'Don't-Know Mind'
Wisdom

Discernment
Being, Not Having

"[In Buddhism] liberation is not of the self, but from the self."[54]

Francesca Fremantle

Right View: Knowing that liberation "from the self" is Buddha's teaching.

Right Thought: Understanding "from the self" means freedom.

Triad 4U: Discernment

In her book *Luminous Emptiness*, Francesca Fremantle succinctly defines the difference between Buddhist teachings and other spiritual teachings. "Liberation of the self" presupposes that if one tries hard enough on the road of self-improvement, one will find freedom from suffering. Instead, Buddha taught that it is our understanding of the self that is the problem, and no amount of self-improvement leads to liberation.

Liberation of the self is the "normal" viewpoint from which most human activity proceeds. First we imagine or perceive ourselves to harbor some imperfection. Then we make plans to overcome the imperfection. Trying to improve ourselves is a worthy pursuit that leads to many benefits for individuals as well as society at large. Development of comfort, convenience, safety, and social issues is enhanced in this way. However, along this path there is no absolute that ensures final contentment. There is no end to desires that are viable candidates for attention. For the individual this means craving without satisfaction, leaving the door wide open for unhappiness and intellectual confusion as well as the possibility of serious mental disturbances.

The underlying assumption of the attempt at liberation of the self is that the self is an object one possesses. Liberation of the self is grounded in a dualistic perspective, one with the subject-object split. Intrinsic to dualistic practice is the idea that a gap exists between one's actual state and a desired state of being.

In liberation from the self, the goal is not perfection; the objective is freedom from the tyranny of self. Liberation from the self allows us to recognize that unresolved conditioned states are like carrying a heavy load. We may not be aware of how much conditioned states impinge on our everyday existence. We are familiar with the continuous stream of psychophysical formations and oftentimes consider them to be who we are even when they

Unfolding of the Eightfold Path

are painful. We value them in spite of the habitual discomfort they inflict. However, when a conditioned state is resolved, we become acutely aware of how burdensome and toxic the afflictive emotions associated with it have been. Setting the load down, we "forget" the pain and open ourselves to an awakened presence.

In the Genjo Koan Dogen says, "To study the self is to forget the self."[55] His term "forget" means to penetrate the core of the self, to learn how to resolve conditioned states, and to understand the complementary relationship of dualities. It is liberation from the self because to "forget" one must become open to the world. If we expect the world to conform to our personal definition, we will suffer dissatisfaction and disappointment. Opening ourselves to the world and accepting the myriad things promotes inspiration and emotional sustenance. The result of forgetting is a balanced and happy person.

Triad 4U – Universal
Establishing 'Don't-Know Mind
Meditation

Immediacy
Thusness

*"At the time of finally forgetting,
there is no duality between the human world and the mountains,
and the present time itself is eternity."*[56]

Zen Master Tenkei

Right Effort: Possessing a calm and courageous will.

Right Concentration: Refraining from attaching to thusness.

Right Mindfulness: Acting from new awareness.

Triad 4U: Immediacy

Immediacy is seeing the heart-to-heart of thusness. The word Immediacy means no middle, the absence of a go-between. Zen Master Tenkei teaches that when the interior relationship of meditation matures, the separation of subject and object dissolves in the nondual presence of eternity. Touching the timeless truth relieves the worry and concern over the body and mind, and "the human world and the mountains" manifest in dynamic stillness.

I heard a talk by Zen Master Dainin Katagiri where he taught that the "za" of zazen means two persons sitting in the vastness. The "za" can literally mean two, or figuratively, any larger number. When two people meet, like a master and disciple, or an individual in relating to an inner teacher, their mutual heritage is a realization outside of time beyond our usual understanding of past, present, and future. Master and disciple or practitioner and his/her life find profound empathy and share a moment of thusness.

Thusness annuls separation and manifests as freedom. Thusness is simple without distortion —we catch sight of something sacred within the mundane. "This something, however, cannot be controlled. It occurs when it occurs. The Zen Master shows in an immediate way how this something can come about when he [comments]: 'The flowers bloom, just as they bloom.'"[57]

Thusness affirms human life in all three modes of practice: zazen, work, and daily encounters. Zazen creates familiarity with the taste of thusness during sitting periods, but the deepest experiences are most often aroused off the cushion. It can happen anywhere. Suddenly, awareness blooms, revealing what is here. Standing on the edge of a cliff in awe and wonder, tears of joy frequently flow. The experience is special, but the Zen Masters advise not to abide there. They wisely counsel to note the newfound knowledge and move on quickly.

Unfolding of the Eightfold Path

The right effort of Immediacy rests in the nondual domain where everything is in its place and nothing is unique. Or is it? Mary Oliver attempts to disregard the ordinary but she fails to do so in the opening lines of her poem *This World*.

> "I would like to write a poem about the world that
> has nothing fancy in it. But it seems impossible."[58]

Mary Oliver's experience is "like a mute person who has had a dream."[59] Encased in thusness, she wants to write something ordinary, but wonder of the world's ordinariness overwhelms her. An enlightenment poem attributed to a lay disciple of Zen Master Chang-tsung echoes her experience. Doubt grew out of the breadth and depth of the disciple's dream and challenged his means to express in words and phrases:

> The sounds of the valley stream his long tongue,
> The changing colors of the mountains his blissful
> body; Since last night I have heard 84,000 hymns,
> But how can I explain them all to people the
> following day?[60]

Triad 4U – Universal
Establishing "Don't-Know Mind"
Morality

Mystery
"Don't-Know Mind"

*"What is known is not much.
What we do not know is immense."*

Pierre-Simon Laplace

*"On the first tree,
The green tree,
Mystery
Created me."*[61]

Archibald MacLeish

*"The uncertain way is the good way.
Upon it lie possibilities.
Be unwavering and create."*[62]

Carl Jung

Right Speech: Exploring the mystery of language.

Right Action: Exploring the mystery of the physical world.

Right Livelihood: Understanding Don't-Know Mind as freedom in action.

Triad 4U: Mystery

As students of the Buddha, only an authentic, direct perception of the truth of life satisfies our yearning. Beliefs, scriptures, deductions, and inferences fall by the wayside, leaving us open to mystery. When asked about it, old clever words pale. What remains is the openness of "Don't-Know Mind"—Laplace's "immense," unveiled by thusness.

Don't-Know Mind is the outcome of the study of reality. It is the middle way of Buddhism where the personal (the mind of discrimination) and universal (the mind of unity) manifest in equal importance.

Studying reality with the mind of discrimination does not produce an understanding of discrimination or unity. An example of this type of study is found in science. When a scientist studies a flower, the flower's constituent parts are separated, categorized, and named. We have labels and an understanding how the flower behaves, but the mystery of the flower's being was left untouched.

However, when studying reality without the mind of discrimination, both the universal mind of reality and the personal mind of discrimination are understood and the flower's totality of being is grasped without recourse to differentiating or labeling.[63]

Laplace's countryman Blaise Pascal described his vision of the world of unknowing, informing us of what remained after the Don't-Know Mind pulled conceptual "certainty" from its pedestal:

> I do not know who put me in the world, nor what the world is, nor what I am myself. I am in a terrible ignorance about everything. I do not know what my body is, or my senses, or my soul, or even that part of me which thinks what I am saying, which reflects on itself and everything but knows itself no better than anything else.... I see

> only infinity on every side, enclosing me like an
> atom or a shadow that vanishes in an instant.

Pascal's vision recounts an entry into a new world. His sense of newness may have been uplifting and exciting, but what emotions surrounded him when facing infinity?

At a conference of precocious child mathematicians, the moderator asked a ten-year-old boy what he thought was the largest number. The boy immediately replied, "390." The moderator asked, "What about 391?" The boy reflected for a moment and said, "I was close."

The boy's response appears simplistic, off the mark, even silly. He could have wisely offered infinity as the largest number, but then as before, someone could have asked about infinity plus one. An endless opinion-driven discussion about the largest number might have ensued. So it mattered little what number he said. However, his "I was close" cut off all arguments.

Don't-Know Mind is like "I was close." Whatever we understand currently is immediately modified in the next moment. What is the largest understanding? It is whatever we understand now, because it is the largest we have. We exist with infinity at all sides and then in the next moment we exist within infinity plus one and so on. Our lives are a constant engagement with the fresh and innovative, even if we are not aware of it. Don't-Know Mind, like Pascal's vision, keeps us open to originality. It motivates the wonder of exploration, deepens the quest for wisdom, and promotes new spheres of compassion.

One objective of zazen retreats is to teach the relationship of right speech and noble silence. Retreats are structured in a non-vocal mode to encourage the growth of internal stillness. Upon a retreat's conclusion, we return to our regular life circumstance and communicate as before. But things are not the same; we have become one with the stillness of Don't-Know Mind. When speaking, we realize that it is noble silence emanating from stillness that animates our everyday speech, showing us that noble silence may be voiced or unspoken. Just remaining silent without stillness is only a lack of words, but speaking within stillness is noble silence.

Right action is rooted in stillness as well. All Zen training endeavors to express stillness in reverential action. The common activities of meals, working, conversing, teaching, studying, and resting are all rooted in stillness.

Right livelihood conforms to social, religious, and intellectual conventions, but with an inner freedom that springs from "Don't-Know Mind." Confidence and trust mark its ventures, even upon entering the strange new land of Don't-Know Mind. Wandering with no apparent destination initiates no trouble. ". . . do not ask me where I am going, as I travel in this limitless world, where every step I take is my home."[64]

Section 5
Refining and Living Liberation
Introduction to Triad 5

"It is only by drawing often, drawing everything, drawing incessantly,
you discover that you have rendered something in its true character."

Camille Pissarro

On the long journey of unfolding the Eightfold Path we encounter diverse experiential landscapes and landmarks both familiar and unexpected. Wisdom progresses from the initial contact of Study to the inconceivability of Discernment. Meditation matures from grappling with the newness of mental discipline to the experience of thusness—Immediacy. The heart of Morality, the Don't-Know Mind of Mystery, breathes life into the precepts, transforming them from guides to direct experience. The Don't-Know Mind finds "you have rendered something in its true character."

The uniqueness of the Buddha's teaching is expressed over and over again in the conversion of our dualistic ideas of the world

Unfolding of the Eightfold Path

into transcendental wisdom in meditation. Meditation, or zazen as Dogen prefers it to be called, is a commitment to move from the first apprehensive steps of Study, to rediscovering Mystery and the freedom of unencumbered activity.

Triad 5 is also a description of a mature practice that combines the personal and universal aspects of experience and displays a holistic understanding of the elements in the previous eight triads. An established Zen life is based on facts, on openness, and eventually results in the freedom of unencumbered activity.

When we explore Sustenance, Wholeheartedness, and Authenticity in our mature practice we are learning to live freedom. We are integrating the change of being realized in Don't-Know Mind. The new morality is based on a transformed state of being. The entire process of the triad can be considered a conscious cultivation and integration of the experience of freedom. It deals with liberation, offering a means by which the emerging experience of freedom can mature and be integrated into all aspects of our life. This confident morality acknowledges the preeminent capability of the freedom and wisdom of Emptiness as the unifying force of the elements united in Triad 5, granting language, reason, artistry, human sentiment, and ethical relations their proper and deserved places as integration proceeds.

Some years after returning from China, Dogen founded Eiheiji Zen Monastery. The monastery was in the mountains near the Sea of Japan, where he led a rigorous practice based on the monastic life he experienced as Zen in China. The monastery had patrons, but most of the time food was at a premium. Zazen was emphasized over sleep during the year-round schedule. Warmth in the cold winters was only intermittently possible. Given these conditions, Dogen formulated his recommendation for the means for a successful life of Zen. His recommendation was to understand

Section 5: Refining and Living Liberation

how food, sleep, and warmth were required in proper amounts. Triad 5 examines how contemporary practitioners can understand Dogen's thirteenth-century advice as Sustenance, Wholeheartedness, and Authenticity, and how these modern equivalencies apply as we integrate Zen teaching into the life of the West.

Triad 5 Refining and Living Liberation
Wisdom – Personal/Universal

Sustenance
Abiding Elixir

"Nirvana is like food. Good food can sustain us and satisfy our hunger. Similarly, nirvana can satisfy all our desires and answer all of our questions."[65]

Zen Master Hsing Yun

Right View: Abiding in facts, not conjecture.

Right Thought: Organizing the life of study upon the psychophysical reality of intention.

Triad 5: Sustenance

Wisdom is the abiding elixir that introduces us to Zen and sustains us as we negotiate the complexities of life. The way may be elusive and ambiguous, but the path of wisdom offers spiritual security. The eight steps of wisdom in triads 1 through 4 describe in part the teachings and experience of growth from conceptual engagement with the Four Noble Truths through liberation from the self. These understandings match Buddha's first and second turnings of the Wheel of Dharma.

The first turning of the Wheel of Dharma took place during Buddha's lifetime. He formulated his initial teachings in a conceptual and logical way using the words and methods of his time. The goal was to show the fleeting interdependent nature of existence, including human life. Analysis of the self could not locate any self-subsistent entity. With no permanent self to defend and perfect, negotiating the path to awakening replaced striving for gain. The moral outcome of Buddha's teaching of no-self, if carried to completion, results in personal liberation. Triads 1 through 3 contain wisdom elements of the first turning.

The teachings underlying the second turning were given by Buddha during his lifetime, passed down orally, and compiled in written form about 500 years after Buddha's death. The second turning taught the direct experience of the oneness of reality, without conceptual mediation. This being the case, liberation is only possible universally—one enlightened all enlightened.

The second turning views the conceptual base of first turning as incomplete. Yet without the ethical basis that the first turning generates, the second turning would be devoid of valid moral principles. Triad 4 describes the transformative powers of the experience of inconceivability of the second turning.

The third turning arose because of the necessity to resolve the conflict between the personal approach of first turning, and

Unfolding of the Eightfold Path

the universal of the second. The third turning focuses on the complementary relationship of concept and immediacy. We are creatures of both thought and experience, made whole in the third turning through the experiential understanding of their interconnection. The third turning facilitates the inner dialogue between the dualistic pairs of our makeup. Triad 5 summarizes the third turning's comprehensive teachings of the resolution of conditioned states, integration of freedom from conditioned states, and living that freedom.

Some years ago, I heard a Zen teacher declare that one should not be in a hurry to start teaching. He advised waiting until you reach the age of sixty before taking on students. Although he did not offer any explanation for how he came to that opinion, I speculate that it is to provide the requisite time for the three turnings and their associated wisdom to mature. Dogen's Zen challenges conventional perspectives, making a lengthy period necessary to fully embody his understanding. Take for example Dogen's famous teaching from the Fukanzazengi, "Think of not-thinking. How do you think of not-thinking?—Nonthinking." At first blush the statement sounds incomprehensible. However, with study, reflection, and time, a different view might emerge. Thinking, not-thinking, and nonthinking could come to be seen as equivalent to the three turnings: thinking as the conceptual beginning, not-thinking as the creative universal mind brought to light by Zen practice, and nonthinking as the inclusive understanding of relationship of the personal thinking with the universal not-thinking.

Master Hsing Yun's quotation suggests that nirvana is the ultimate sustenance, nurturing the whole person; all sides of our nature must be sustained for overall well-being. Ignoring any need can weaken our health. The Zen life requires vigor and stamina. A lifestyle that promotes fitness should be established and maintained.

Triad 5: Sustenance

A holistic approach to ensuring our vitality and endurance includes nurturing five aspects of our being:

1. **Physical Well-being:** To sustain physical well-being, a diet of appropriate nutritious food, and a consistent program of exercise are necessary.

2. **Emotional Health:** Understanding the nature of afflictive emotions and their inner and external effects is essential for eliminating barriers to healthy, mutually fulfilling relationships.

3. **Intellectual Stimulation:** Developing a habit of lifelong learning using all available methods to develop paths to wisdom, including cultivation of creative ways to receive and communicate knowledge, and promote thoughtfulness and rationality.

4. **Psychological Maturity:** Maturity is attained when we acquire the expansive ability to approach both psychological and spiritual issues with skill and confidence.

5. **Spiritual Understanding:** Wisdom is our essential nourishment. Without it, malnutrition of the heart occurs from deficiency in the basic human need of awakening. Master Hsing Yun suggests a healthy helping of nirvana. The right view of Sustenance rests on the growth of wisdom from along the path from Study to Discernment.

In right thought, the five aspects of personal nourishment receive day-to-day attention with an honest appraisal of physical, intellectual, and spiritual nutritional needs.

Triad 5 Refining and Living Liberation
Meditation – Personal/Universal

Wholeheartedness
Openness

"The antidote to exhaustion is not necessarily rest."
"Then what is it?"
"The antidote to exhaustion is wholeheartedness."[66]

David Stendahl-Rast and David Whyte

Right Effort: Exercising the right thought of nonthinking.

Right Concentration: Creating wholeheartedness within the Formal Posture—Informal Mind

Right Mindfulness: Manifesting wholeheartedness within the Formal Mind—Informal Posture

Triad 5: Wholeheartedness

A Zen teacher once observed that practitioners come to retreats and the first thing they realize is how exhausted they are.[67] She contended that exhaustion is born of our modern American life that shatters our inherent wholeness of being into pieces. No amount of rest, as it is normally thought of, has the ability to put the pieces back together. However, when one simply sits down on the meditation cushion, the cure begins to show itself: "The antidote to exhaustion is wholeheartedness."

Pleasure and work are often thought of as opposites. Like many other dualities we have observed, a second look at their relationship is necessary to view the entire picture. Wholehearted activity leads to energy; it also leads to a life where work and leisure are not two separate events. Cultivation of wholeheartedness is not found only in leisure. It arises from an awareness of the wonder of ordinary things and events of the world.

I learned the meaning of wholeheartedness during a series of seven-day sesshins I attended in the 1980s. Special teaching did not bring it about; rather, it arose within the normal flow of events of the sesshins.

The same priest presided over all of the retreats. His instruction style included walking around during sitting periods adjusting posture when required, and offering relief from shoulder tension and refreshment through the use of the kyosaku stick. I became dependent on his watchful eye to ensure my body was upright, and to the shoulder blows to reinvigorate my efforts to stay aware. Then, one sesshin, without explanation, the priest stopped his attentive rounds and remained on his cushion. I was left on my own without help, feeling abandoned and a little angry.

I soon realized the foolishness of blaming the priest for my weaknesses and eventually gained the ability to sit straight with a continuity of awareness without his aid. I realized that my dependence

Unfolding of the Eightfold Path

on the teacher had caused an internal split. His aid had become a hindrance. Without the "assistance" of his change, I might not have found the way to self-reliance and a wholehearted approach to zazen practice.

Wholeheartedness within the confines of a sesshin is easy because of the controlled environment. Stepping away from that supportive environment can test the strength of any realization. The story below highlights the life of an individual who demonstrated an exemplary insight into how to accomplish wholeheartedness even when placed in situations of extreme emotional stress.

I met an elderly Japanese woman at a temple event in 1972. Her name was Miyoko and she was seventy-two at the time. We became friends, and I would stop at her house occasionally to drink tea. I greatly enjoyed her gregarious humor. It was fun to be with her and listen to her stories. Over the months, little by little her life story emerged.

Miyoko came to America as a mail-order bride for a Los Angeles fisherman when she was nineteen. Prejudice against Asians was rampant in Southern California, especially during World War II. She and her family were interned for three years during the war. Upon release, the family found that their fishing boat was sold, and another family had taken over their house. They lost everything and had to start over from the beginning.

I was curious about how she achieved an attitude free of resentment and bitterness in spite of the constant bias, imprisonment, and theft of her home and business property. I asked how she was able to go beyond hard feelings. She said, "Life is life, war is war, peace is peace, and I go on day-to-day." The simple statement does not convey the depth of her meaning; that was contained in the intensity of her gaze. Miyoko fully lived her life, discarding grudges, transforming the negativity heaped on her into wholehearted mindfulness.

Triad 5: Wholeheartedness

In the practice of zazen we experience wholeheartedness and seek to embody its attributes. Four attributes of wholeheartedness are:

1. Zazen generates wisdom and compassion by recognizing emptiness and interdependence of life.
2. Zazen is a creative refuge in a world splintered by the afflictive emotions of conditioned states.
3. The major focus of practice is the integration of the mind, body, and breath in zazen, and then learning how to bring that inner accord to all aspects of everyday life.
4. Daily meditation engages with the fruit of spiritual practice described by Dogen as "repose and bliss."[68]

We rediscover our natural state of wholeheartedness when we learn how to cherish the primacy of a unifying thought amidst the fragmenting tumult of conventional living.

Triad 5 Refining and Living Liberation
Morality – Personal/Universal

Authenticity
Freedom

With freedom, books, flowers and the moon,
who could not be happy?

Oscar Wilde

Right Speech: Recognizing language as a liberating experience. Responses develop and are expressed in a way that is consistent with the immediate requirements of the moment.

Right Action: Responding with an open heart-mind. Confidence and trust are the hallmarks of personal, intrapersonal, and interpersonal skills.

Right Livelihood: Realizing that authentic personhood is Zen's ethical contribution to society.

Triad 5: Authenticity

During retreats Katagiri Roshi would often say how rare it was to have the opportunity to practice together. Listeners to his comments on this subject speculated on what he meant. Some of the conclusions were:

- Religious freedom is uncommon. One should appreciate the chance to practice freedom of choice.
- Rare it is to encounter the Dharma and understand and value it when it is presented.
- Rarer is the occurrence that among the countless beings of the universe that these particular people would be here at the same moment of time and place and practice zazen together over many days.
- Rarest it is to embody and manifest the Dharma.

These four items match Oscar Wilde's conclusion "who could not be happy?" The retreat participants had the freedom of religious choice, the education of many writers through books as well as the living Dharma of Katagiri Roshi, the "flowers" of companionship, and the moon of practice/realization that Dogen taught as "complete fulfillment."[69]

Authentic personhood manifests in Zen practice as our participation in the growth of the precepts. When a practitioner sets off on the Zen path the precepts alert him to what is regarded as right speech, right action, and right livelihood. The meaning of the "right" elements changes as practice matures.

Right speech—refraining from lies or slander—is our initial understanding that develops into experiential knowledge of language as liberation. Human language is rooted in discriminating thought, expressing itself in words and sentences. In Zen practice, language combined with the awareness of zazen transforms confused thinking into right thinking. Articulation of the words and sentences

Unfolding of the Eightfold Path

of discriminating thought removes the bonds from discriminating thought. Language, it can be said, liberates discriminating thought where disordered thinking changes to clarity of vision. Right speech naturally arises from redeemed discriminating thought, showing itself in accuracy of articulation, rapport with conditions, and caring inflection. Language, with its many-faceted nuances, communicates the unknown in each utterance. Right speech originates in the depth of being and flows out with wonder and mystery.

Authentic right action is the intention of behaving in a way that promotes the welfare of others. The needs of others are the central motivation in our daily pursuits. They are most often small acts, performed with a spontaneity that comes about when a need is observed.

One day, a young Japanese monk who was that day's Jisha waited while the abbot mounted the sitting platform. When the abbot pulled his feet out of his slippers, the monk picked them up and put them in their proper place. The monk's intention was service, and his intent was without equivocation. The sweetness of Zen practice is touched off by active sensitivity.

The question of what constitutes authenticity of right livelihood in Zen has been around since its inception. Many attempts have been made over the centuries to clarify the question with uncertain results. In seventeenth-century Japan two contending views arose, each sponsored by notable teachers. Manzan Dohaku espoused that "transmission from master to disciple" as described in Dogen's *Face-to-face Transmission* was authentic Dharma. Tenkei Denson advocated that the understanding of enlightenment—a profound grasp of the nature of reality—can arise under innumerable circumstances, and should take precedence over the master-disciple relationship.[70]

In the world of administrative institutions, the debate is unsolvable. Yet each Zen practitioner individually confronts this two-sided issue. Is authenticity gained and verified by a teacher, or by self-validation in the encounter of the self with the living reality of awakening?

Perhaps the realization of the truth of this question resides in action. Master Hsing Yun says, "Sharing the dharma is the highest form of generosity."[71] In his view, authentic personhood is expressed in selfless service no matter how one comes to it.

Right livelihood includes the following. For most of us, some of these characteristics are in nascent form, requiring gradual cultivation to bring about authentic living:

- Having a job that contributes to the social order.
- Meeting and regarding fellow beings with acceptance.
- Connecting with and sharing the benefits of spiritual insight.
- Seeing the whole world as one's own and responding accordingly.
- Honoring cultural and societal norms and being aware of how they benefit life.
- Living freely, apart from the domination of conditioning; enjoying the all-inclusive existence of unencumbered activity.

Authenticity is the experience of the universal mind that illuminates all beings. It basks in being one with the whole. Attaining this mind, one can act with proper attunement. It exhibits its rectitude in the following ways:

- The exclusive and dualistic positions of the nihilistic view of nothingness and the permanent self of eternalism are avoided. Taking the inclusive Middle Way invites all beings to find freedom from argument and hatred.

- One has confidence in interpersonal skills, performing shared daily tasks with alacrity, self-reliance, heart-to-heart relations, and conviction.
- Creative contributions are made to the well-being and growth of the community of Buddhists: the Sangha is enjoyed as a refuge.
- Engagement with the larger community and growth of an expanded sense of responsibility that develops out of the vision that all beings are rooted in the core of universal truth.

We find the key to right livelihood in Zen Master Yun-men's teaching on our commonality of nature. He addressed his assembly:

> "Every person has a radiant light without exception…. What is everybody's radiant light? No response came from the audience. So he spoke for them: The monastics' hall, the buddha hall, the kitchen pantry, the main gate."[72]

The radiant light within every human is ours alone yet shared with all beings, animate or inanimate. Whatever activity we are engaged in, whatever beings we encounter, the radiant light marks our lives with an intimacy that manifests in all directions. Allowing its truth to flow into the world is the ultimate benevolence we can offer others.

Eightfold Path Summary

Radiant Light of the Buddha
Exists throughout the Dharma world.
Homage to the countless Buddhas in the ten directions,
Permeating hearing and seeing manifesting Nirvana.[73]

At the center of Buddhism lies the profound teaching of the intricate relationship of the radiant light of the Buddha. The radiant light, or radiance of mind and the clarity that issues forth from its embodiment, exists at the very core of all beings. Within this radiance our deepest yearnings find satisfaction. We cannot avoid it even if we want to, because its being penetrates the entire Dharma world. Isolation and alienation drop away with the realization of how interdependent all beings really are. Attaining a personal enlightenment is really not possible. Not one step along the path can be taken without saving all beings and being saved by all beings.

Shakyamuni Buddha taught the Eightfold Path and left it for us to map the terrain by personally learning what wisdom, meditation, and morality mean to us as our life unfolds. Each of us is given the task to create a structure of study and practice within

Unfolding of the Eightfold Path

the particulars of our situation, directly experiencing the heart of the teaching. The triads are a description of one point of view, presenting topical information in one of many possible forms. They are offered as a means for reflection and insight.

In the *Sutra of Forty-Two Chapters*, the Buddha summarized the Eightfold Path in this way:

> My doctrine is to think the thought that is unthinkable, to practice the deed that is not-doing, to speak the speech that is inexpressible, and to be trained in the discipline that is beyond discipline. Those who understand this are near; those who are confused are far. The Way is beyond words and expressions, is bound by nothing earthly.[74]

Endnotes

Introductory quote
1. Thomas Cleary, *Classics of Buddhism and Zen* Volume 4 (Boston: Shambhala Publications, 2005) p. 240.

Preface
2. The Four Noble Truths are: 1) Suffering arises. 2) Suffering arises from causes and conditions. 3) The causes of suffering can be resolved. 4) Freedom from suffering is attained by following the Eightfold Path.

Chapter 1 The Eightfold Path Chart
3. The Eightfold Path is commonly divided into these three categories. The Western philosophical terms of epistemology, ontology, and ethics come close to the Eastern meanings of wisdom: knowing how to know; meditation: knowing how to experience reality; and morality: knowing how to express reality. However, Buddhism adds to Western conceptual understanding with its adherence to the teaching of lived experience. The reader will find additional information on the categories later in this chapter and throughout the book.

Chapter 2 Commentaries on the Triads
4. Morality in this study does not refer to behavior based on commandments or set rules. Rather, Morality means speech, action, and living that springs up from an intimate interconnection and relationship with the source of inherent purity discovered within the practice of meditation.
5. Robert Buswell, *Tracing Back the Radiance* (Boston: Shambhala Publications, 1983) p. 99. The quote is from Zen Master Chinhul's writing entitled Secrets on Cultivating the Mind.

Unfolding of the Eightfold Path

Triad 1P: Study

6. Each triad commentary has a definition block in the upper left-hand side of the first page of the commentary that has the triad number, what teaching section and category it is, and whether it is personal or universal aspect.
7. Eihei Dogen, "Actualizing the Fundamental Point" [1233], ed. Kazuaki Tanahashi. *Moon in a Dew Drop* (San Francisco: North Point Press, 1985) p. 69.
8. See William H. Thomas, *What Are Old People For?* (Acton, MA: VanderWyk & Burnham, 2004) p. 127 for a diagram that approaches study-karma-liberation in meaning. Thomas offers a modern-day example to the ancient idea of study-karma-liberation. Thomas' pattern of childhood-adulthood-elderhood includes transition periods of adolescence between childhood and adulthood and senescence between adulthood and elderhood. It offers an analysis of the transitions, describing senescence as "human ripening." He brings in the self-actualization of Maslow, but the enlightenment of the East is not specifically mentioned. Nonetheless, the similarities to liberation are apparent and elderhood is valued as a creative period and a culmination of a life fully lived.
9. Eihei Dogen, "Actualizing the Fundamental Point" [1233], ed. Kazuaki Tanahashi. *Moon in a Dew Drop* (San Francisco: North Point Press, 1985) p. 69.

Triad 1P: Practice

10. Shunryu Suzuki, *Zen Mind, Beginner's Mind* (New York: Weatherhill, 1970) p. 31.
11. Dainin Katagiri, *Returning to Silence* (Boston: Shambhala Publications, 1988) pp. 167–172. See "The Art of Zazen" for his description of the integration of the body, breath, and mind in zazen.

Triad 1P: Ethical Conduct

12. This version of the precepts was compiled and distributed by Zen Mountain Monastery, Mt. Tremper, New York.
13. Dainin Katagiri, *Returning to Silence* (Boston: Shambhala Publications, 1988) p. 95.
14. Text of Bodhidharma's version the Ten Grave Precepts comes from the Sydney Zen Centre, Sydney Australia.

Endnotes

Triad 1U: Spiritual Autonomy
15. Kalamas Sutra

Triad 1U: Absolute Equality
16. Francis Cook, *Hua-yen Buddhism* (New York: Pennsylvania State University, 1977) p. 118.
17. Aldo Leopold, *A Sand County Almanac* (Oxford, U.K.: Oxford University Press, 1949) p. xxvi.
18. Ibid, p. xxi.
19. Kosho Uchiyama, trans. Shohaku Okumura and Taigen Dan Leighton, *The Wholehearted Way* (Boston: Tuttle Publishing, 1997) p. 23. Quote is from the translation of Zen Master Dogen's Bendowa, a section of which is known as the Jijiyu Zammai, chanted daily in Zen training centers.

Triad 1U: Intimacy
20. Dainin Katagiri Roshi, *Each Moment Is the Universe* (Boston: Shambala Publications, 2007) p. 142.
21. Thomas Cleary, *Secrets of the Blue Cliff Record* (Boston: Shambala Publications, 2000) p. 60.
22. Zen Master Dogen, *Jijiyu Zammai*, Ryumonji Zen Monastery Chant Book.

Triad 2P: Questioning
23. Thomas Cleary, (Boston: Shambhala Publications, 1989) p. 1.
24. Conditioned states are deeply rooted psychophysical formations predicated by negative experiences. They are how we store negative learning. They arise as a way to mitigate difficult life events, but continue to influence our experience and behavior long after an event is over. A complex of afflictive emotions accompanies conditioned states, as well as habitual thought patterns and behaviors. They limit our freedom to respond to our life in ways we might prefer. A great deal of energy is expended in coping with conditioned states. See Tending the Fire: An Introspective Guide to Zen Awakening by Dale and Barbara Verkuilen for a full treatment of conditioned states and how to alleviate them.

Unfolding of the Eightfold Path

Triad 2P: Impartiality

25. Mu Soeng, *Trust in Mind* (Boston: Wisdom Publications, 2004) p. 13.
26. Zen Master Dogen, *Fukanzazengi*, Ryumonji Zen Monastery Chant Book.
27. Ibid
28. Ibid

Triad 2P: Relating

29. Hee-Jin Kim, *Dogen on Meditation and Thinking: A Reflection on His View of Zen* (Albany, NY: SUNY Press, 2007) pp. 1–2.

Triad 2U: Introspection

30. Hsing Yun, *Describing the Indescribable* (Boston: Wisdom Publications, 2001) p. 131.
31. Hee-Jin Kim, *Dogen on Meditation and Thinking: A Reflection on His View of Zen* (Albany, NY: SUNY Press, 2007) p. 96.

Triad 2U: Insight

32. Andy Ferguson, *Zen's Chinese Heritage* (Somerville, MA: Wisdom Publications, 2000) p. 369.
33. Zen Master Tung-shan Liang-chieh, *Song of the Jewel Mirror Awareness*, Ryumonji Zen Monastery Chant Book.
34. Eihei Dogen, *Dogen's Extensive Record: A Translation of the Eihei Koroku*, translated and edited by Taigen Dan Leighton and Shohaku Okamura (Somerville, MA, Wisdom Publications, 2010) p. 288.

Triad 2U: Interconnection

35. John Daido Loori, *Bringing the Seed to Life* (Boston: Shambhala Publications, 1999) p. 43.
36. Quoted by David Loy in *The Great Awakening: A Buddhist Social Theory* (Somerville, MA: Wisdom Publications, 2003) p. 193.
37. Zen Master Dogen, *Fukanzazengi*, Ryumonji Zen Monastery Chant Book.
38. Francis Cook, *Hua-yen Buddhism* (New York: Pennsylvania State University, 1977) p.2.

Triad 3P: Personal Orientation

Endnotes

39. Walker, Alice, *The World Will Follow Joy* (New York: The New Press, 2013) p.xv
40. Welwood, John, *Toward a Psychology of Awakening* (Boston: Shambhala Publications, 2000) pp. 12–13.

Triad 3P: Interpersonal Orientation

41. Steven Heine, *The Zen Poetry of Dogen* (Boston: Tuttle, 1997) p. 37.
42. Eihei Dogen, Fukanzazengi, Ryumonji Zen Monastery Chant Book.

Triad 3U: Psychological Maturity

43. Shantideva, trans. by Vesna A. Wallace and B. Allan Wallace, *A Guide to the Bodhisattva Way of Life* (Ithaca, NY: Snow Lion, 1997) p. 1.
44. Thanks to Paula Hirschboeck, Zen priest and retired Professor of Philosophy at Edgewood College, Madison, Wisconsin for this image.

Triad 3U: Embracing

45. Chant recited in the morning by Zen practitioners.
46. Tung-shan Liang-chieh, *Song of the Jewel Mirror Awareness*, Ryumonji Zen Monastery Chant Book.

Triad 3U: Dignity

47. Eihei Dogen, trans. by Taigen Leighton and Shohaku Okumura, *Dogen's Pure Standard for the Community* (Albany, NY: State University of New York Press, 1996) p. x.
48. John O'Donohue, Beauty–*The Invisible Embrace* (New York: HarperCollins, 2004) p. 31.

Section 4: Establishing Awareness of "Don't-Know-Mind"

49. Steven Heine, *The Zen Poetry of Dogen* (Boston: Tuttle, 1997) p. 102.
50. See "Songs for Eve," a group of poems that communicate Archibald MacLeish's understanding of the change from naïve experience to the self-aware. A. MacLeish, *New and Collected Poems 1917–1976* (Boston: Houghton Mifflin, 1976) pp. 437–457.

Unfolding of the Eightfold Path

Triad 4P: Inevitability

51. Shinkichi Takahashi, composer of the poem was a twentieth-century Japanese philosopher and poet. Quoted by Lucien Stryk in *Awakening*. (Athens, OH: Swallow Press Books, 1981) Dedication.
52. An anonymous person penned this on a bookstore copy of the Full Earth photo.

Triad 4P: Intergrating

53. Soyu Matsuoka Roshi, *The Kyosaku* (Atlanta: Atlanta Zen Center, 2006) p. 210.

Triad 4U: Discernment

54. Francesca Freemantle, *Luminous Emptiness* (Boston: Shambala Publications, 2001) p. 37.
55. Eihei Dogen, "Actualizing the Fundamental Point" [1233], ed. Kazuaki Tanahashi, *Moon in a Dew Drop* (San Francisco: North Point Press, 1985) p. 69.

Triad 4U: Immediacy

56. Thomas Cleary, *The Secrets of the Blue Cliff Record* (Boston: Shambala Publications, 2000) p. 110.
57. Ueda Shizuteru, "Wisdom and Language in Meister Eckhart and Zen Buddhism," *The Eastern Buddhist* (Volume XXIV, No. 1, Spring, 1991) p. 73.
58. Mary Oliver, *This World from Why I Wake Early* (Boston: Beacon, 2004) p. 27.
59. Robert Aitken, *The Gateless Gate: The Wu-men Kuan* (New York: North Point Press, 1991) p. 9.
60. Steven Heine, *The Zen Poetry of Dogen* (Boston: Tuttle, 1997) p. 169.

Triad 4U: Mystery

61. A.MacLeish, *New and Collected Poems* 1917–1976 (Boston: Houghton Mifflin, 1976) p. 455.
62. Jung, Carl, "Red Book" (New York: W.W. Norton, 1991) p.625
63. See Red Pine, *The Zen Teachings of Bodhidharma* (New York: North Point Press, 1987) p. 55 for an expanded explanation of this point.
64. Steven Heine, *The Zen Poetry of Dogen* (Boston: Tuttle, 1997) p. 61.

Endnotes

Triad 5: Sustenance
65. Zen Master Hsing Yun, *Lotus in a Stream* (Trumbull, CT: Weatherhill, 2000) p. 134.

Triad 5: Wholeheartedness
66. David Stendahl-Rast and David Whyte in conversation on David Whyte's Sounds True compact discs entitled *Clear Mind Wild Heart.*
67. This comment was made by Zen teacher Linda Somlai of the Original Root Zen Center of Racine Wisconsin at a retreat in Madison, Wisconsin in 1998.
68. Zen Master Dogen, *Fukanzazengi*, Ryumonji Zen Monastery Chant Book.

Triad 5: Authenticity
69. Eihei Dogen, trans. Kosen Nishiyama and John Stevens, Shobgenzo, *The Fascicle of Tsuki, the Moon* (Sendai, Japan: Daihokkaikaku, 1975) pp. 83–85.
70. Heinrich Dumoulin, *Zen Buddhism: A History*, Japan (New York: MacMillan, 1990) p. 336.
71. Hsing Yun, *Describing the Indescribable* (Somerville, MA: Wisdom Publications, 2001) p. 106.
72. Urs App, trans. Master Yunmen: from the *Record of the Chan Master* "Gate of the Clouds" (New York: Kodansha International, 1994) Number 143.

Eightfold Path Summary
73. Katagiri Roshi recited this verse to himself as he offered incense during services and at private occasions as well. It is from the Ryaku Futatsu Repentance Ceremony, Ryumonji Zen Monastery Chant Book.
74. Zen Master Soyen Shaku, *Zen for Americans* (La Salle, IL: Open Court, 1906) p.1. Part of Chapter 18 of *The Sutra of Forty-Two Chapters.*

Bibliography

Abram, David. *The Spell of the Sensuous*. Toronto: Random House, 1996.

Aitken, Robert. *Original Dwelling Place*. Washington D.C.: Counterpoint, 1996.

Batchelor, Stephen. *Alone with Others*. New York: Grove Press, 1983.

Bielefeldt, Carl. *Dogen's Manuals of Zen Meditation*. Berkeley: University of California Press, 1988.

Chang, Garma C. C., *The Hundred Thousand Songs of Milarepa*. Boston: Shambhala, 1999.

Cleary, Thomas. *Secrets of the Blue Cliff Record*. Boston: Shambhala, 2000.

———. *The Secret of the Golden Flower*. New York: HarperSanFrancisco, 1991.

———. *Zen Lessons*. Boston: Shambala, 1989.

Cook, Francis. *Hua-yen Buddhism*. London: The Pennsylvania State Press, 1977.

Dumoulin, Heinrich. *Zen Buddhism: A History, India and China*. New York: Macmillan, 1994.

———. Zen Buddhism: *A History, Japan*. New York: MacMillan, 1990.

Ferguson, Andy. *Zen's Chinese Heritage*. Somerville, MA: Wisdom, 2000.

Fremantle, Francesca. *Luminous Emptiness*. Boston: Shambhala, 2001.

Green, J. *The Recorded Sayings of Zen Master Joshu*. Boston: Shambhala, 1998.

Unfolding of the Eightfold Path

Hagen, Steve. *Buddhism Plain and Simple*. New York: HarperCollins, 1999.

Heine, Steve. *The Zen Poetry of Dogen*. Boston: Tuttle, 1997.

Hixon, Lex. *Living Buddha Zen*. Burdet. NY: Larsen Publications, 1995.

Hsing Yun. *Core Ideas*. New York: Weatherhill, 2002.

———. *Lotus in a Stream*. New York: Weatherhill, 2000.

———. *Describing the Indescribable*. Somerville, MA: Wisdom, 2001.

Johnson, Will. *The Posture of Meditation*. Boston: Shambala, 1996.

Katagiri, Dainin. *Returning to Silence*. Boston: Shambhala, 1988.

———. *Each Moment is the Universe*. Boston: Shambhala, 2007.

Kim, Hee-Jin. *Dogen on Meditation and Thinking*. Albany, NY, SUNY Press, 2007.

Leighton, Taigen and Okumura, Shohaku. *Eihei Koroku*. Boston: Wisdom Publications, 2004.

———. *The Whole Hearted Way*. Boston: Tuttle, 1997.

Leopold, Aldo. *Sand County Almanac*. New York: Oxford Press, 1949.

Low, Albert. *The Butterfly's Dream*. Boston: Tuttle, 1993.

Loy, David. *Non-duality*. New York: Humanity Books, 1988.

MacLeish, Archibald. *New and Collected Poems*. Boston: Houghton Mifflin, 1976.

Matsuoka, Soyu. *The Kyosaku*. Atlanta: Atlanta Soto Zen Center, 2006.

Mu Soeng. *Trust in Mind*. Boston: Wisdom Publications, 2004.

O'Donohue, John. *Beauty – The Invisible Embrace*. New York: HarperCollins, 2004.

Oliver, Mary. *Why I Wake Early*. Boston: Beacon Press, 2004.

Pine, Red. *The Zen Teachings of Bodhidharma*. New York: North Point Press, 1989.

Popper, Karl. *The Open Society and its Enemies*. Princeton, NJ: Princeton University Press, 1962.

Bibliography

Powell, William. *The Record of Tung-Shan*. Honolulu: Kuroda Institute, 1986.

Price, A. *The Sutra of Huineng*. Berkeley, CA: Shambala, 1975.

Rahula, Walpola. *What the Buddha Taught*. New York: Grove Press, 1959.

Shaku, Soyen. *Zen for Americans*. La Salle, IL: Open Court, 1906.

Stryk, Lucien. *Encounters with Zen*. Athens, OH: Swallow Press, 1981.

Suzuki, Shunryu. *Zen Mind, Beginner's Mind*. New York: Weatherhill, 1970

Tanahashi, Kazuaki. *Enlightenment Unfolds*. Boston: Shambhala, 1999.

—————. *Moon in a Dew Drop*. San Francisco: North Point Press, 1985.

Verkuilen, Dale and Barbara. *Tending the Fire: An Introspective Guide to Zen Awakening*. Madison, WI: Firethroat Press, 2012.

Von Durckheim, Karlfried. *Hara*. London: Unwin Paperbacks, 1962.

Walker, Brian. *Hua Hu Ching*. New York: HarperSanFrancisco, 1992.

Welwood, John. *Toward a Psychology of Awakening*. Boston: Shambhala, 2000.

Glossary

Some of the terms listed below are common Buddhist vocabulary; others are expressions specifically conceived or adapted for this text.

Abhidharma: The analysis of what constitutes the self. One of the three basic teachings of "small vehicle," the others being the sutras and the monastic rules.

Acceptance: Also termed Equanimity. Seeing and living without separation between oneself and others.

Arahat: One who is free of worldly fetters and who has achieved personal enlightenment.

Ango: Zen training period lasting from 30 to 90 days.

Barriers: See Conditioned States.

Bodhidharma: Founder of Zen in China in the sixth century C.E.

Bodhisattva: The ideal of Mahayana Buddhism. One on the path toward enlightenment. One who after achieving enlightenment dedicates her/his life to helping others on the spiritual path.

Brahma Vihara: The pure abodes of Kindness, Compassion, Sympathetic Joy, and Acceptance.

Unfolding of the Eightfold Path

Conditioned States: Also referred to as Karmic Obstructions. Conditioned States are psychophysical formations that are habitual responses predicated by past events that limit our freedom to respond to the present. They have a negative emotional tone. There is an awareness that we are not responding as we might wish to. A great deal of energy is expended coping with karmic obstructions, but coping strategies do not alleviate the underlying cause of the automatic response.

Buddhadharma: The teachings of the Buddha; universal truths.

Dependent Origination: Also termed Co-dependent Origination and Dependent Co-origination. Phenomena do not have an independent permanent existence. They are produced by a combination of ever-changing causes and conditions.

Dogen: Thirteenth-century Japanese Zen Master who transmitted Soto Zen to Japan after a period of study in China. Author of the Shobogenzo and numerous other works.

Dukkha: First of the Noble Truths, it is often translated as "suffering arises." Looked at from a wider perspective, however, dukkha consists of the direct experience of the human situation with all its complexities.

Dharma Seals: The Dharma Seals are impermanence, lack of a self-nature (no permanent self), and Nirvana. They are said to possesses the four characteristics of ultimate truth: they are universal, necessary or inevitable, true in the past, and true in the future.

Duality: Thinking based on the assumption that there is a gap between the subject (thinker) and an object (what is thought about).

Eightfold Path: The Fourth Noble Truth, the path to the cessation of suffering. Consists of eight aspects: right view, right thought,

Glossary

right effort, right concentration, right mindfulness, right speech, right action, and right livelihood. See Eightfold Path Charts for detailed information.

Emptiness: The central teaching of Mahayana that everything is impermanent and lacks a permanent self-nature.

Formal Mind: In sitting meditation a continuity of awareness is developed. The Formal Mind of Right Mindfulness is this continuity in action. The Informal Mind of sitting is a mind without boundaries, one that lets all mental elements exist within the stream of awareness. The Formal Mind of movements in the world maintains a continuity of awareness of all physical activities. The Informal Mind focuses on a mentality without boundaries for the inner world; the Formal Mind focuses on a mentality without boundaries for the outer world. Awareness of each movement is kept with a minimum of distraction; when distraction does occur, awareness is returned to the moment without judgment of the distraction.

Formal Posture: The Formal Posture is the bedrock of meditation practice. Applying this correctly opens the door to concentration. The Formal Posture of sitting meditation uses a cushion that promotes straight-back sitting. Although this posture may seem arbitrary, practicing it will reveal the vigor, intensity, and the comfort that is its nature.

Four Noble Truths: The fundamental teaching of Buddhism: The Truth of Suffering, The Truth of the Origination of Suffering, The Truth of the Cessation of Suffering, The Truth of the Path to the Cessation of Suffering.

Gassho: A gesture where the palms are placed together in front of the face expressing the unity of life experienced in meditation practice.

Hara: Located in the lower belly. Manifests as the foundation of sitting meditation, the physical and energetic embodiment of the original life center.

Impermanence: A Dharma Seal that says each and every phenomenon changes from one moment to the next.

Informal Mind: The Informal Mind is without definition. It is relaxed and alert. In it, mental formations come and go without judgment, but with an awareness of their passing: a limitless mentality. Its practice consists of tranquility and insight. Tranquility grows out of the continuity of awareness achieved over time. Insight occurs spontaneously within the sphere of tranquility. Neither need be sought. They naturally arise within the consistent persevering Right Effort of meditation practice.

Informal Posture: The Informal Posture is our daily life actions within the awareness of Formal Mind. The practice of Informal Posture consists of physical movement and engagement with the world at large permeated with tranquility and insight. The continuity of awareness of sitting becomes the ordinary mind of walking. With practice, the mind of sitting becomes the Formal Mind that is at the heart of the liberated activities of Informal Posture.

Karma: The action of the law of cause and effect: all intentional or volitional acts are causes that engender a subsequent effect. Karma created in the past by our spiritual and physical ancestors is inherited and forms the foundation of our life. We could say in actuality our personal situation is the sum total of the entire universe acting out as our life, at this particular point in space, in this particular moment of time. We thus conclude the personal and the universal are one – our personal karma is identical to universal karma.

Glossary

Karmic Obstructions: See Conditioned States

Katagiri, Dainin, Roshi: (1928–1990) Founder of Minnesota Zen Meditation Center and Hokyoji Practice Center. Taught in the United States from 1963 to 1990.

Kinhin: Walking meditation practiced between periods of zazen.

Liberated Activity: Activity free of karmic obstructions.

Mahayana Buddhism: Known as the "great vehicle" because its ideal is to bring all beings to enlightenment. The Bodhisattva embodies its three main teachings of emptiness, interdependence, and that all phenomena express universal truth.

Matsuoka, Soyu, Roshi: (1912–1997) Founder of the Chicago and Long Beach, California Zen Centers. Taught in the United States from 1939 to 1997.

Meditation: One of the three divisions of the Eightfold Path. Also see Zazen.

Mondo: The recorded exchange between a Zen Master and student, often initiating the awakening of the student.

Morality: One of the three divisions of the Eightfold Path. Moral action in Buddhism is the natural expression of the success in negotiating the elements of the Eightfold Path. The precepts are the guideposts to Buddhist rectitude and attunement. See Triad 1P Ethical Conduct.

Natural Koan: Inquiry is the very essence of Buddhist meditation practice out of which the awareness of an individual's Natural Koan arises. An individual's Natural Koan, their personal spiritual dilemma, contains both the obstructions to progress and the

Unfolding of the Eightfold Path

answer and means to resolve them. Asking questions and learning to trust the responses that form and arise from the depths of being refine the understanding and functioning of the Natural Koan.

Nirvana: The Dharma Seal that expresses freedom from suffering

Nonduality: Realization that there is no gap between the subject (thinker) and an object (that thought about).

Okesa: The robe of Buddha depicting a rice field representing the cultivation of mind, worn by monks and nuns.

No permanent self: The Dharma Seal that states all beings are devoid of an independent and permanent self-nature. All beings depend on all other beings for the causes and conditions in which their existence is rooted.

Personal and Universal aspects of self: Synonyms for personal are individual, relative, difference, and conventional; synonyms for universal are collective, absolute, unity, and ultimate. One might suppose that the universal is more important, but this is not the case. The elements are of equal value. Both must be studied and made one's own. Learning the personal without the universal deprives one of the fullness of the Buddha's insight. Attempting to learn the Universal without a firm grounding in the personal limits one's ability to sustain the benefits of a breakthrough. Without the universal, the personal tends toward the moralistic and scholastic; without the personal, the universal lacks warmth and stability. The two aspects are really one seamless effort, but they are put into categories in order for the conceptual mind to think and speak about them.

Prajna: Wisdom that comes with the recognition of nonduality.

Glossary

Precepts: The Buddhist precepts are not the equivalent of the commandments of Judaism and Christianity. They do not attempt to impose restrictions on behavior given by some outside authority, nor are they moral imperatives. When first encountering the precepts most Westerners can hardly stop from seeing them in the moral sense; our ways of thinking on these matters are deeply ingrained. However, working with the precepts, and witnessing our lives unfolding within them, the effects of the teachings slowly penetrate our pursuits. The precepts are transformed from moral dictates into a living and breathing awareness of the Buddha mind. The precepts are descriptions of the world of the Buddha, enlightenment expressed in daily life.

Spiritual Bypassing: A common but mistaken response to the discomfort and dissatisfaction of daily life. In spiritual bypassing, problematic emotional and personal issues are left unresolved, while spiritual practices are used to find release from the pain associated with them.

Suzuki, Shunryu, Roshi: (1904-1971) Founder of the San Francisco Zen Center. Taught in the United States from 1957 to 1971.

Thusness: The direct experience of emptiness as the true nature of reality.

Tung-shan Liang-chieh: [Tozan Ryokai (Japanese)] Ninth-century Zen Master whose life and teaching are the basis of the Soto Zen school.

Triads: Nine descriptions of the three divisions of the Eightfold Path—Wisdom, Meditation, and Morality—that illustrate the penetration of Zen teaching within a practitioner's perseverant effort.

Unfolding of the Eightfold Path

Twelve Links of the Chain of Causation: Explains the causes and conditions that underlie the cycle of birth and death.

Wisdom: One of the three divisions of the Eightfold Path. Knowledge of the Buddha Mind.

Zazen: A single-minded effort of seated meditation that seeks no gain and whose mental sphere is objectless and imageless. See Informal Mind above.

The Eightfold Path Charts

Full size color copies of the Eightfold Path Charts are available as a free download at www.firethroatpress.com/downloads

Unfolding of the Eightfold Path

Section 1 **Foundations of Zen Buddhist Practice**

	Wisdom Right View, Thought
Triad 1P–Personal	**Study**
	Reading/Reflecting/Reasoning
Personal Aspect of Foundations	Right View: Directly experiencing the validity of the Four Noble Truths.
	Right Thought: Forming the intention to gain experiential understanding of Buddha's teaching of awakening.

Triad 1U–Universal	**Spiritual Autonomy**
	Alone in the World
Universal Aspect of Foundations	Right View: Understanding the nature of personal responsibility.
	Right Thought: Recognizing Emptiness as the medicine that resolves the adverse effects of conditioned states.

Section 2 **Inquiry as the Central Point of Practice**

	Wisdom Right View, Thought
Triad 2P–Personal	**Questioning**
	Conditioned States
Personal Aspect of Inquiry	Right View: Valuing the dilemmas that our life situation brings to us.
	Right Thought: Placing questioning at the center of our practice.

Triad 2U–Universal	**Introspection**
	Forms of the Natural Koan
Universal Aspect of Inquiry	Right View: Realizing that what is searched for, and what satisfies that search, is within the Mind.
	Right Thought: Acquiring knowledge of the Natural Koan and forming intentions based on that knowledge.

The Eightfold Path Charts

Section 1 — Foundations of Zen Buddhist Practice

Meditation Right Effort, Concentration, Mindfulness	**Morality** Right Speech, Action, Livelihood
Practice Discipline	**Ethical Conduct** Precepts
Right Effort: Applying the will in an appropriate, useful, and consistent manner.	Right Speech: Refraining from lies or slander, using appropriate timing, not being harsh or insulting, cultivating kindness.
Right Concentration: Learning about our inner makeup and how to deal with its complexities. Learning and applying the principles of Formal Posture – Informal Mind.	Right Action: Establishing and maintaining daily activities to promote the health and welfare of oneself and others.
Right Mindfulness: Applying the learning from the meditation practice into the world of daily activities. Learning and applying the principles of Formal Mind – Informal Posture.	Right Livelihood: Engaging in work that does not harm others.

Absolute Equality Alone in the World with All Beings	**Intimacy** Rapport with All Beings
Right Effort: Intentionally acting in a way that recognizes that all life is interdependent and equal.	Right Speech: Using words and tone of voice that acknowledge the power of everyday communication.
Right Concentration: Acknowledging the birth of compassion for oneself.	Right Action: Practicing and performing our daily pursuits within the awareness of the needs of others.
Right Mindfulness: Acknowledging the birth of compassion for others.	Right Livelihood: Expressing our commonality of being within our occupations, family lives, and other endeavors.

Section 2 — Inquiry as the Central Point of Practice

Meditation Right Effort, Concentration, Mindfulness	**Morality** Right Speech, Action, Livelihood
Impartiality Balance without Preference	**Relating** The Key Question of Dualistic Interplay
Right Effort: Putting aside the mundane concerns of daily life at the onset of zazen practice.	Right Speech: Articulating words and phrases that penetrate, clarify, and liberate thought.
Right Concentration: Allowing conditioned states to become apparent within the Informal Mind.	Right Action: Cultivating nonduality of mind makes the needs of others central.
Right Mindfulness: Observing with the Formal Mind the effects of conditioned states in everyday relationships.	Right Livelihood: Noticing how closeness manifests when the path to nonduality is established.

Insight Receptivity	**Interconnection** Nature of Unity with All Beings
Right Effort: Learning how to use the mundane as an integral part of practice.	Right Speech: Connecting speech with insight.
Right Concentration: Learning to trust the unity of inquiry and response.	Right Action: Connecting actions with insight.
Right Mindfulness: Carrying the source of insight into the world.	Right Livelihood: Allowing the openness of Emptiness to express itself as connection with others.

Unfolding of the Eightfold Path

Section 3 **Cultivating Psychological Well-being**

	Wisdom Right View, Thought
Triad 3P–Personal Personal Aspect of Well-being	**Personal Orientation** Basis of Practice
	Right View: Understanding the form and timing of the work required for spiritual practice. Engaging with the self with utmost dignity; understanding the nature of roles and rules.
	Right Thought: Nurturing a balanced focus toward life that understands the danger of trying to solve problems through spiritual gain.

Triad 3U–Universal Universal Aspect of Well-being	**Psychological Maturity** Stability
	Right View: Witnessing the hand-in-glove activities of the so-called internal and external worlds of human experience.
	Right Thought: Relying on Buddha's teaching of Dependent Origination.

Section 4 **Establishing Awareness of "Don't-Know Mind"**

	Wisdom Right View, Thought
Triad 4P–Personal Personal Aspect of Establishing "Don't-Know Mind"	**Inevitability** Recognition of the Human Condition
	Right View: Witnessing events without embellishment.
	Right Thought: Being face-to-face with the inconceivable: the unthinkable and implausible are always before us.

Triad 4U–Universal Universal Aspect of Establishing "Don't-Know Mind"	**Discernment** Being, not having
	Right View: Knowing that liberation "from the self" is Buddha's teaching.
	Right Thought: Understanding "from the self" means freedom.

The Eightfold Path Charts

Section 3 — Cultivating Psychological Well-being

Meditation Right Effort, Concentration, Mindfulness	**Morality** Right Speech, Action, Livelihood
Intrapersonal Orientation	**Interpersonal Orientation**
Progress	Accomplishment
Right Effort: Recognizing achievement and change, and using that knowledge to overcome resistance to practice.	Right Speech: Experiencing satisfaction with simple controlled discourse.
Right Concentration: Cultivating lighthearted pleasure and contentment within the Informal Mind.	Right Actions: Practicing restraint in conduct mirrors the Formal Mind.
Right Mindfulness: Establishing satisfaction and an attitude of delight as a fact of life within Informal Posture.	Right Livelihood: Responding to the world's needs with a sense of personal responsibility. Trying to find the edge of what we consider "our life."

Embracing	**Dignity**
Acceptance	Worthiness
Right Effort: Finding energy and encouragement in a deepening understanding of the self.	Right Speech: Being aware of how trust and confidence can manifest in tone and word choice.
Right Concentration: Practicing with poise and self-reliance, undeterred by the presence of conditioned states.	Right Actions: Being aware of how trust and confidence can manifest in all manner of physical expressions.
Right Mindfulness: Internalizing the negative effects of conditioned states.	Right Livelihood: Cultivating the insight that the whole world is ours. Trying to find the edge of what we consider "our responsibility."

Section 4 — Establishing Awareness of "Don't-Know Mind"

Meditation Right Effort, Concentration, Mindfulness	**Morality** Right Speech, Action, Livelihood
Clarifying	**Integrating**
Without Lack	Seamless Serving
Right Effort: Making a wholehearted attempt at plumbing the point of connection with impermanence.	Right Speech: Speaking, like chanting, is accomplished by listening.
Right Concentration: Relinquishing the anxiety of desire to have, to gain, and to do better. Exploring the boundaries of the Informal Mind freed from the limits that desire imposes.	Right Actions: Acting, like walking meditation, is done with harmony of attention and body movements.
Right Mindfulness: Cultivating satisfaction and an attitude of delight within the Informal Posture. Exploring the boundaries of the Informal Posture freed from the limits that desire imposes.	Right Livelihood: Recognizing and serving the needs of others to awaken.

Immediacy	**Mystery**
Thusness	"'Don't-Know Mind'
Right Effort: Possessing a calm and courageous will.	Right Speech: Exploring the mystery of language.
Right Concentration: Refraining from attaching to thusness.	Right Actions: Exploring the mystery of the physical world.
Right Mindfulness: Acting from new awareness.	Right Livelihood: Understanding Don't-Know Mind as freedom in action.

Section 5 — Refining and Living Liberation

	Wisdom Right View, Thought
Triad 5	**Sustenance** Abiding Elixir
	Right View: Abiding in facts, not conjecture.
	Right Thought: Organizing the life of study upon the psychophysical reality of intention.
Attributes of Refining and Living Liberation	Physical well-being Emotional health Intellectual stimulation Psychological maturity Spiritual understanding

The Eightfold Path Charts

Section 5 — Refining and Living Liberation

Meditation Right Effort, Concentration, Mindfulness	**Morality** Right Speech, Action, Livelihood
Wholeheartedness	**Authenticity**
Openness	Freedom
Right Effort: Exercising the right thought of nonthinking.	Right Speech: Recognizing language as a liberating experience. Responses develop and are expressed in a way that is consistent with the immediate requirements of the moment.
Right Concentration: Creating wholeheartedness within the Informal Mind—Formal Posture.	Right Actions: Responding from an open heart-mind. Confidence and trust are the hallmarks of personal, intra-personal, and interpersonal skills.
Right Mindfulness: Manifesting wholeheartedness within the Formal Mind—Informal Posture.	Right Livelihood: Realizing that authentic personhood is Zen's ethical contribution to society.
Ensuring a balanced practice with proper respites Integrating body, breath, and mind Creative relationships with dualistic pairs Familiar with the method of resolving conditioned states	Avoidance of extremes Confidence in interpersonal skills Intimate engagement with the Sangha of Buddhists Intimate engagement with the universal community Life is grounded in seamless serving

Other offerings from Firethroat Press
www.firethroatpress.com

The Tale of Zen Master Bho Li by Barbara Verkuilen is an original story of an eight-year-old orphan who becomes a beloved Zen Master. Evocative themes are deftly conveyed through endearing characters in this beautifully illustrated winsome Zen fable.

Dokusan with Dogen: Timeless Lessons in Negotiating the Way by Barbara Verkuilen is the wisdom of Master Dogen combined with modern scientific findings, Zen lore, and contemporary Zen anecdotes, providing a unique blend that is entertaining and informative.

Tending the Fire: An Introspective Guide to Zen Awakening by Dale and Barbara Verkuilen is an in-depth study of the awakening process that blends Master Dogen's teaching of radical nonduality with an original Western psychological perspective on transformation.

Where the Dragon Meets the Water: The Founding of Ryumonji Zen Monastery edited by Dale Verkuilen is the written and oral record of interviews with six key individuals involved in the spiritual and physical establishment of Ryumonji.

Words within Silence by Joe Kyugen Michaud. Kyugen's 108 poetic offerings explore the various ways in which we approach

Unfolding of the Eightfold Path

the truth, picking the lock of our entrapment, opening our imagination, and delivering us to freedom.

Lost Time by Joe Kyugen Michaud. Kyugen follows up his previous work, Words within Silence, with another 108 poems that are vehicles of intimate communication. He invites the reader to accompany him as he delves into the mystery of thusness.

Study Guides and Free Downloads Firethroat Press also offers a selection of study guides and essays on various Zen topics.

About the Author

Taizen Dale Verkuilen has been studying Zen Buddhism since 1968. He lived at the Long Beach, California Zen Center and was ordained in 1970 by Soyu Matsuoka Roshi. After ten years he pursued a career in business, continuing his study as a lay practitioner with Dainin Katagiri Roshi. He was re-ordained in 2000 by Shoken Winecoff Roshi, Abbot of Ryumonji Zen Monastery.

He and his wife, Renshin Barbara Verkuilen, also a Zen priest, founded the Midwest Soto Zen Community in Madison, Wisconsin in 2001. Taizen is the co-author with Renshin of *Tending the Fire: An Introspective Guide to Zen Awakening*.